MAYORDOMO

MAYORDOMO

Chronicle of an Acequia
in Northern New Mexico

STANLEY CRAWFORD

UNIVERSITY OF NEW MEXICO PRESS
Albuquerque

This book has won the 1988 Western States Book Award for Creative Nonfiction. The Western States Book Awards are a project of the Western States Arts Federation. The awards are supported by the Xerox Foundation, Waldenbooks, and Crane Duplicating Service. Additional funding is provided by the National Endowment for the Arts Literature Program.

Library of Congress Cataloging-in-Publication Data

Crawford, Stanley G., 1937–
    Mayordomo: chronicle of an acequia in northern New Mexico / Stanley Crawford.—1st ed.
        p. cm.
    Bibliography: p.
    ISBN 0-8263-0999-2
    1. Irrigation water—New Mexico—Management. 2. Irrigation canals and flumes—New Mexico—Maintenance and repair.   3. Water—New Mexico—Distribution—Management.   I. Title.
    TC824.N6C73   1988
    333.91'3'09789—dc19   87-24487
                                                                 CIP

Design: Milenda Nan Ok Lee

For My Mother and Father
and in Memory of Alister Brass

So the river is a god

Knee-deep among reeds, watching me
Or hung by the heels down the door of a dam

It is a god, and inviolable.
Immortal. And will wash itself of all deaths.
—Ted Hughes, from River

Contents

Preface: Words and Names

One cannot speak or write about the community irrigation ditches of New Mexico without using the Spanish terminology of their physical and organizational structure, if one is to do justice to them. The Spanish vocabulary that inhabits the following account roughly corresponds to that which I normally use in my dealings with my own ditch and would be common to others who are actively part of a ditch association in northern New Mexico, whether their first language is Spanish or English.

The term *acequia,* which can refer to both the actual irrigation channel and to the association of members organized around it, derives from the Arabic *as-saquiya.* Each *acequia* is individually governed by a *comisión* of three landowner *parciantes,* or member-shareholders. *Parciantes* are assessed in work or money and obtain water from the *acequia* according to the size of their plots of land in terms of *piones,* from *pión,* worker, also meaning by extension "share," a local variant on the more standard *peón.* Usually elected by the *parciantes* along with the *comisión,* the *mayordomo* is the ditch manager and is usually paid a monthly salary during the irrigation season. The approximately one thousand *acequias* of New Mexico vary in size from several *parciantes* to over one hundred.

The following account covers a year in the life of a small *acequia* in northern New Mexico, from March 1985 to March 1986. In it, I have changed all local place and personal names in order to protect the privacy of the community, which should not be interpreted as sign of ingratitude toward my fellow *parciantes,* commissioners, *mayordomos* who have confided to me, admonished me, and guided me over the past nineteen years.

This book would not have been written without the unflagging encouragement of Gus Blaisdell. Also, I owe thanks to Elizabeth C. Hadas of the University of New Mexico Press for her patience and understanding, and to Clark de Schweinitz of Northern New Mexico Legal Services for helping me clarify numerous points of water use and water law over many years; and to Rose Mary Crawford, always my foremost reader, companion *parciante* through it all: words, water, mud, and sky.

April 1987

One

We have been at work nearly an hour this windless spring morning, an aura of haze at the horizons promising no more than brief gusts later in the day, in the afternoon, when it will be hot. I am standing on a bank overseeing a row of men bent double as they dig. Mutterings and grunts pass up and down the line, the clang of shovel blades, the clack of handles, the hiss of dry brush being pushed or kicked away. I lean on a six-foot length of a slightly curved cottonwood branch that tapers from two inches in diameter where I hold it between my hands to less than an inch thick at the lower end with which I scratch a series of lines across the irrigation ditch every fifteen minutes or so to mark the divisions between *tareas*. Long, deep cracks run the length of the weathered staff, yet it is strong, having already served the year before for this same purpose. I note that the older men below me, and the oldest would be over seventy, know how to keep their shirts tucked in while the youngest, the fifteen- and sixteen-year-olds in outgrown clothes, expose strips of backside in varying shades of whiteness and brownness, smoothness, hairiness. I will know that they are all finished with their sections, their *tareas,* even the men beyond the bend and hidden by the willows, when I hear the clamor ceasing of shovels splashing into gravel. There will be silence, a few laughs, and then I will hear putty knives scraping mud from the blades, and the sound of files singing against metal.

Fewer workers have shown up than I expected this Saturday morning, only seventeen. We had thirty yesterday. We still have the most difficult part of the ditch to dig, a half-mile from here to the lower *desagüe.* The seventeen-year-olds flash their mirrored sunglasses at me, wondering if I will be hard on them and make them dig *una pal' abajo* deep like the woman *mayordoma* Juliana Espinosa does on the other side of the river, or whether I will be satisfied with a cursory scraping of dry grass off the lower edges of the banks. Her son, a blustery insecure kid of sixteen or so, is back working again today despite some words between us yesterday. I hear someone say: "They all went out and got drunk." "Who?" I call down from the bank. "The ones who got paid yesterday?" "Yeah," someone else calls out. Laughter. The pay is low, $2.50 an hour, a dollar below the minimum wage,

$20.00 a day, but enough to buy some gas for the car and an evening of beer drinking. Last night was a full-moon Friday. Our missing thirteen *piones* are sleeping it off. Fewer *piones* means more hours of work but also harder digging for everyone. When your crew is over thirty in number, then you seem to spend more time walking and taking breaks than shoveling. But I am not one of those who will work our small crew half to death to prove something—that we are men or that this is work or that I am in charge. The ditch itself will pace our labors. As it winds its way, the Acequia de la Jara, through thickets of willow and plum along this stretch of particularly luxuriant growth above Gregory Serna's overgrown apple orchard, I know where most of the weak spots are in the bank and where they will have to be built up and where the grass has grown constrictingly thick and where the channel must be widened a little, and there will be enough sandbars to shovel out on the inside of bends along the serpentine course: this will be the work that proves enough to tire my workers by the end of the day. And almost anything we do will serve to keep the ditch wide and deep enough to accept the rolling tongue of water, clogged with leaves and twigs, muddy and white foamed, that will race down the three-foot-wide channel two days from now, Monday, the twenty-fifth of March, 1985, from one end to the other of the twisting watercourse, through a culvert under a highway, down through a siphon under an arroyo, along the backyards of some twenty houses and across the high ground back of empty fields and neglected orchards, until the water finally fans out over a pasture and spreads out through a grove of cottonwoods and willows to trickle back into the Rio de la Junta, rejoining the waters it was separated from by a small diversion dam two miles upstream.

I move on down the line. The bank stands a good three feet above the ditch channel along here before dropping off precipitously into Gregory's orchard ten feet or so below, and is overgrown with willows and wild rose canes. As I make my way along the crown of the bank inspecting my workers' *tareas* I must watch my footing. It will not do to slip off and disappear down into the brush below. Lose footing and lose face. I pause above Juliana's son, Frankie, whom I regard with suspicion—he keeps his eyes on me too insistently—and reach down and draw a line with my staff along a ridge of grass-sprinkled silt he well knows he should have dug out. "Square it up along there." His neighbors to either side look down at their own *tareas* and poke at clumps of mud with the tips of their shovels. I move on down the line. The bank lowers and becomes less treacherous. This is the most difficult section of the irrigation ditch. Along here it runs ten to twelve feet above three little-used bottom-land fields, hugging a south-facing hillside which is the source of a fertile clay soil that supports an abundant growth of willow, wild rose, New Mexico olive, squawberry bush, native plum, hemlock, *oshá,* clovers and alfalfa, and innumerable types of grass. The day before yesterday, Thursday, ten of us with long-handled pruning shears took two passes through here at cutting back last season's growth in order to clear standing room for us to dig today. The clay soil is also the favored habitat of burrowing creatures, both muskrats and crayfish, which excavate systems of tunnels underneath the channel and carve small drains here and there in the south bank. What starts out as a trickling leak in the side of the ditch can end up in a major collapse in which ten to twenty feet of bank slides away into the orchard below. This has happened once or twice a year now for the past five years. Each time the *mayordomo* must summon a crew of ten men or so to dig out a new channel further back into the hillside. We repaired one such collapse yesterday at the end of the day, a gaping cave-in that had stood there all winter since last October. Two feet down in the red clay of the new channel we had sliced into the hillside were the thin strata of carbon perhaps from some ancient brush fire. Perhaps this stretch of the *acequia* has always been difficult: perhaps a hundred years ago they cleared the brush away with fire, as we did the year before last. Or two hundred years ago. Nobody knows how old the Acequia de la Jara is. Reynaldo Vasques, a former *mayordomo* now in his sixties, says it was here in the time of his grandfathers. Now and then it seems strange to me that such things—community irrigation ditches, *acequias*—survive these days, despite what I sense as a decline in the subsistence agriculture that first brought them into existence. I cannot imagine, knowing what I now know, the immense labor that would have brought even this one into existence, small as it is, a channel that varies from four feet to a foot and a half in width in its two miles of wanderings through the back yards along the side of the hills. The first Spanish settlers could have dug the Acequia de la Jara as early as 1750, perhaps using forced labor from a nearby Indian pueblo. By comparison this present time must be a pleasant, comfortable dream. With one or two exceptions, the men and boys are working today for a little extra money, not out of necessity.

They stand below me now pausing for breath, glancing up at me for some signal. They begin to turn, shuffle along the channel, kick at the fine sand.

"*¡Vuelta!*" I call out. "*Vamos.*"

They file past me, sound of shovel blades dinging as the metal brushes against twigs. A canopy of dry brown willow branches, old growth standing dead in place, arches over the ditch. This first day of spring sees nothing in green beyond the occasional trefoil leaf of clover or alfalfa peeping out from beneath dry leaves. At the edges of fields and along fencelines the new-growth willow twigs have deepened in orange, and on cottonwood and native plum, buds are beginning to swell. The landscape ripens, glowing, toward spring; following the next storm, whose currents will assist the vultures on the last leg of their soarings up from Mexico where they winter, the wind, that great seed-dispersing machine, will blow for days on end from midmorning until dusk. The winds have been so far subdued this year. We have often had to dig out the ditch in gale winds, through brush and trees alive with creaking movement. The sand and silt blows into your eyes and ears and mouth, lodges in your hair, under your collar. But today the light of the morning remains soft and mellow, and I think the day will remain mercifully calm. Two of the older men, the cousins Orlando and Ewaldo Serrano, have rolled cigarettes. The scent of tobacco hovers over the line as it moves, shuffling, toward the next section, bent backs to me as I fall in behind them, with their old denim jackets, faded flannel shirts, white T-shirts on the kids used to the cold from waiting for the morning school bus, and then they pause to turn their faces back toward where I stand, the heavy-lidded and broad faces of the older Serrano men, Indianlike with their high cheekbones and full lips, the grey eyes of Reynaldo Vasques always ready to smile or show irritation or anger, a small-boned man with finely cut features and who seems to have scarcely aged in the nearly fifteen years I have known him.

The *tareas* I normally measure out are perhaps two paces long, five or six feet, making a section, a *vuelta,* between eighty and a hundred feet long with a crew this size. This is only my second season as *mayordomo*, but I have walked the ditch as a *parciante* and as a member of the *comisión* for fifteen years, enough times that the annual cleaning, *la limpia* or *la saca*, has come to mark the line between winter and spring perhaps as surely to me as those who have grown up with the custom. I was thirty-two when I moved here. My first year as a *parciante*, owner of an empty field of willow-covered bottomland my wife and I had bought the previous autumn, I stumbled out of bed like a nervous teenager the morning of my first ditch cleaning and wondered where I had left the shovel and whether I should file it sharp, worried over what clothes to wear, wondered if the weather was going to be warm or cold that day, whether the wind would come up and spoil the slowly accumulating heat of the first days of spring—and feared that I would be unable to keep up with the others in my digging or that I would be confused by the counting in Spanish. That first year in the early 1970s I worked under the stern eye of Reynaldo Vasques, then *mayordomo*, my number *catorce* today, who would often jump down from the bank and grab my shovel and hack into the side of the ditch with it to show where he wanted the channel *más ancho*, wider, wider. . . . That was the only year I worked as a *parciante*, digging awkwardly, spasmodically, wearing myself out by digging too deeply alongside those who had done

8

such work every spring since they were fourteen or fifteen or were tall and strong enough to handle a shovel and had early mastered the art of digging out just enough, not a shovelful more, to convince the inspecting eye of the *mayordomo* that they have done the necessary work—the *mayordomo* being more likely to pass a *tarea* that looks clean and is neatly scraped of dead leaves and dry grass and rocks than one that has been actually dug out but remains messy-looking. The following year I was elected to the *comisión* of three at the annual meeting in the dusty village schoolyard where those of us who became the *comisión* nearly outnumbered the voting *parciantes* present. Commissioner, *comisionado*, is an imposing title bestowing only the privilege of exemption from the physical labor of digging out the ditch during the March cleaning. I was elected, if that is the word, to become a petty bureaucrat who would drive around collecting money from some twenty-some suspicious neighbors. "You should make those people pay, the *delincuentes*," I was told again and again.

And there were other reasons. I soon discovered that the *parciantes* of the Acequia de la Jara had managed to divide themselves into two feuding factions, the two Vasques families who lived at the bottom end of the ditch, and everybody else. Jerry Munster, another newcomer gringo elected to the *comisión* that year, was at first as flattered as I was at the honor bestowed on us by the Serranos, who outnumbered the

Vasqueses at the meeting. Reynaldo, however, remained as *mayordomo* and persisted through that year
in sending his second youngest son, Randy, around to
collect money—the joke circulating at the time held
that whenever Randy needed to work on his Chevy
he would make the rounds shaking down *parciantes*.
Such practices had perhaps earned the family the ill
will of their neighbors, who responded by letting as
little water as possible pass down to the end of the
ditch. Reynaldo and his wife Teresa were very secre-
tive with the ditch books; whenever you went to their
place to find out how much you owed in *delincuencias*
or *mayordomia,* they disappeared into a back room.
Fifteen minutes later they would emerge with a scrap
of torn-out notebook paper with a figure scrawled on
it. The new commission never obtained the ditch
books but within a year or so, after consulting with
officials of other ditches, we awoke to the obvious
impropriety of a *mayordomo* collecting money to pay
his own salary. We set up a new bookkeeping system,
began collecting the money ourselves and paying the
mayordomo a monthly salary for the six-month season, an arrangement Reynaldo accepted after an initial
period of distrust and as soon as he realized that it was
easier to come to the treasurer for a monthly check
than drive around to argue with his neighbors. He
was a good *mayordomo* for spring cleanings, though
during the irrigation season he tended to neglect the
ditch unless he actually needed water down at his

place; much of the time the ditch ran lower than it might have.

I shuffle along behind the crew and note a stretch of bank that has barely been scraped of weeds and not dug at all, a roll of silt and mud that should have been dug out. I will have to inspect the next section more thoroughly. They grumble if you work them too hard. But they'll grumble if you don't work them hard enough, don't do a good job: they grumble for the ditch. You have to show them that you can be forceful when it is necessary for the ditch to be so. I reach the end of the dug-out section. Ahead lies a sandy white stretch of meandering ditch littered with leafless orange willow clippings and straw-colored stalks of dry clover. As I place my right foot on the border that marks the dug from the undug, the crew stops and turns to watch me pace out their *tareas,* wondering whether their numbers will fall where they are now standing. I place the tip of my staff in the sand about two paces ahead of my right foot and draw it across the width of the channel and call out: "*¡Uno!*" The *pión,* who has slipped in behind me, moves into my place as I step forward and immediately begins hacking at the growth of grass and clover along the sides of the channel. "*¡Dos!*" If I have marked well, my right foot comes down on the line. Two paces. A *tarea,* a job or chore, long enough to work well without banging elbows with your neighbors. "*¡Tres!*" And the same length, if possible, as the ones next to it on either side, longer or shorter exceptions to be made at fencelines, culverts, or other irregularities.

As a commissioner I used to arrive the morning of cleanings to help the *mayordomo* check in the *parciantes* or *piones* working for them, a complex task when thirty people show up to work for themselves or for a neighbor, plus another ten or fifteen men from the village who have come looking for work, plus a carload who have driven down from the nearest mountain village, some of whom can be assigned to a *parciante* who has neither shown up nor sent a *pión*—plus the usual latecomers, *parciantes* or *piones,* who had heard that the digging was going to start at the bottom of the ditch, not at the top, or at the top end, not at the bottom, or who arrive with pruning shears when they should be bringing shovels or shovels when they should have brought pruning shears. Men must be reassigned or sent away for the proper tools or sent away without work or to find a *parciante* who will pay them to work for him at the end of the day. In the old days, if there were old days, the *parciante* himself showed up, or a son or cousin, everyone knew who was working for whom, and the record keeping would have been no more complex than determining who among invited guests had or had not arrived for a party. The absentees, the *delincuentes,* were then assessed for the time of their absence at an hourly rate determined by the commission at the annual meeting, then as today. These sums, plus the monthly *mayordomia* collected to pay the *mayordomo*'s salary for the irrigation season, constituted the *acequia*'s modest treasury.

For ten years as a commissioner I helped the three preceding *mayordomos* check in crews each morning during the spring cleaning which could last from two to four days. But I brought along a shovel, too, and afterward tagged along to clean up sections of the ditch which in my estimation had not been well enough dug out. What, they may have wondered, is this innovation? A *comisionado* who digs, who comes along behind us and tells us with this digging that we do not know how to do our job? And worse, a *gabacho. . . .* (This bewildering epithet was once applied to French refugees in seventeenth-century Spain and is thus historically appropriate to the Anglos who sought refuge in the Hispanic villages of northern New Mexico from the turbulence of urban America in the late 1960s and early 1970s.) The first year of my tagging along, the last day of the cleaning, a cold and windy afternoon in March, the then *mayordomo* Reynaldo Vasques, *pión* number fourteen today, looked at his watch and handed me the willow pole of his office, *la vara,* said, "I have to take my wife to the doctor," and left me in charge of a crew of twenty old men and boys and fellows in their late twenties whom I regarded as hoodlums and near criminals. Some of them had been drinking. Sand blew into the air every time someone lifted a shovel. For all I knew, the first time since the Conquest the *tareas* were being counted out in English. One of the *piones* stole away, one of the end ones, number one or two, getting his neighbor to dig his *tarea* so he could run down to his pickup and then drive down to the bar for some more beer. I remained calm and collected in the face of possible insurrection, at least in appearance. The reigning tough, Johnny Castillo, boozer, frequent wrecker of cars, bar fighter, much the same age as I was, took to sneaking up behind me and bringing his shovel blade down on a nearby rock with a jarring bang, ostensibly to dislodge mud from it, to titterings among the crew. After the second or third bang, I kept my eye on him. I wondered whether I was to be beaten up, whether they would continue their drinking at the bottom of my drive through the night, light bonfires, shoot off guns. Fears. To come home one night to find flames and black smoke billowing out of the windows of the adobe house my wife and I were building. It had happened to newcomers to the mountain villages.

"*¡Y diecisiete!*" I draw the line for the last *tarea*. Benny Romo brushes past me to assume his position to dig. "Excuse me," he says. He's eighteen or so, arrives in the cold morning wearing a tank top and no jacket, and I am told he picks fights with anyone he regards worthy of his interest, Chicano or Anglo.

Mop of black hair, sallow skin, short and compact body, he comes from a family on another ditch up the river, the father probably a maintenance worker at Los Alamos National Laboratory fifty miles away. With his neatly pressed khaki pants and black work boots, cracked but polished, not Levis, not cowboy boots, Benny wears the uniform of his class. He's among the latest crop of tough kids in the valley. Luck or circumstances are likely to carry him toward an early marriage, kids, too many kids, but maybe a good-paying construction job, a mobile home in town or back of his parents' house—or the drinking and the fighting can become a career of sorts and lead toward a collision on the highway between two and six on a Friday or a Saturday morning or shots in the darkness, in the moonlight, in a driveway, in an arroyo, at the side of the road, and all the rest. To me this morning he says, "Excuse me." I am too old to fight—nearly fifty, gangly, tall, a *gabacho,* a likely enemy but exempt by age. He warns me of two low strands of rusty barbed wire that lie across the ditch at knee level just as I am about to walk into them. "Watch out for the wire," he says. I thank him. He moves into the center of his *tarea* and begins working away silently, carefully. I marvel at his respect. I never have to ask him to re-dig his *tarea.* I don't need to. The tough kids do their work without being asked, as a matter of pride.

I climb up on the bank. A tangle of roses and willows litters my prospective path. I steady myself with my cottonwood staff as I feel my way along the bank and call out, "Wider along here," and occasionally pause in order to thrust the tip of the pole down into the ditch among legs and shovels and draw it along a shoulder of silt or grass or a sandbar I want dug out. "Square it up along there." I crash through the brush. I inspect the whole line. This time everyone is to feel the weight of my authority. Or lightness. I am still uncertain this morning how to pace our time. This is our last day. The workers who most count on the money are anxious about how long we are going to work. "You think it's gonna take us all day? Think we'll be done by noon?" I'm not sure. In any case I will slip them a half hour or an hour here and there, break early for lunch, tack an extra hour on to their time this afternoon if we finish early. I am less anxious for their goodwill than I once was, but feel that the pay has slipped below what it ought to be. At $2.50 our ditch is progressive in relation to some ditches in Taos, which still pay the minimum wage of around 1950. The hourly rate is commonly voted on at each ditch's annual meeting in December or in the spring, and if the ditch is controlled by elderly retiree *parciantes,* then $1.25 an hour is likely to be considered a good wage—but in 1985 no one but young babysitters will find it acceptable. Low pay means that *parciantes* won't bother to show up to work on a ditch,

16

and no one will much care if the spring cleaning takes three or four or five days except those who actually have to clear the brush and dig out the dirt and who will finally do so mostly for other reasons. Over the years I have come to feel a certain gratitude for those who actually show up, however broken-down or hungover or for whatever mercenary reason; and I come closest to despising those able-bodied land-owners who neither come themselves to dig nor send their spoiled sons—and later complain to me about paying someone a dollar below the minimum wage to work for them. Land around here is worth above ten thousand dollars an irrigated acre. It costs in labor two or three days per *pión,* per share, to obtain a share of water from the ditch for the six-to-eight-month season it is running, plus about thirty dollars a season for *mayordomia,* to pay my salary of one hundred dollars a month, again per share. Roughly seventy dollars a season if you pay it all in money, contributing no labor. This gives you the right to have water flowing in abundance in ditches all over your property once a week or so, or a smaller trickle almost continuously day and night for six to eight months. Seventy dollars a year, a hundred at most during a bad year when we have problems at the dam, makes the difference between what you see above the ditch on the north side of the valley, a hillside, a glacial dumping of small boulders and gravel and sand through which push here and there outcroppings of red clay, and a sparse growth of stunted piñon pines and junipers and patches of grama grass, little islands of faded green and tan that often live from April to August from a few drops of rain—and what you see to the south, the downside of the ditch, where apple trees grow and alfalfa fields, vegetable gardens, chile and corn patches, rows of grapes, small fields of garlic and wheat, dense thickets of willow and native plum, *bosques* of cottonwood that pump out fine sprays of nearly invisible mist in the hottest days of late June, and water rushing out of ditch gates into feeder ditches, into the veins and capillaries, the irrigation rows, to flood the green fields.

That is, unless the fields have been neglected or abandoned. On our ditch, which irrigates perhaps seventy acres of bottomland, I would say that over half the land is no longer used. Only two of us come anywhere close to making a living off the land now. Reynaldo Vasques, the old *mayordomo,* my number fourteen today, working away down there despite a hernia and a heart condition and who still plows his chile field with a horse, and me up here, current *mayordomo,* over-educated novel-writing truck farmer who lives a life (I sometimes think) caught between two eras like a character in a Turgenev novel.

"¡*Vuelta!*" I call out. "*Vámanos.*" One by one, the crew bends down to enter the canopy of willows that overarches the next section.

Along here the ditch has a good slope and, even though it snakes back and forth to follow the contour of the hillside and thread its way through a stand of large cottonwoods, it accumulates little sand or silt. The bottom is spread with a layer of small gravel washed clean of sand. It does not have to be dug out. Only the sides need be scraped of grass and perhaps widened slightly where there are no thick roots. Next year we should spend some time along here cutting back the growth of willows whose uppermost branches, living and dead, intertwine themselves above our heads. With my pole I mark out long *tareas*. "Scrape the sides along here." I won't inspect this section. The field below is rarely used anymore beyond pasturing an occasional horse. It belongs to Larry Bustos, who lives several fields up on the Acequia de los Cerritos and who served as a commissioner and then as *mayordomo* on our ditch for several years. Though young at the time, he was a responsible commissioner and I could fault only his habit of carrying a loaded .45 on the seat of his pickup whenever we went out collecting *delincuencias* together at night. "You never know what you're going to run into," he once told me when I remarked something to the effect that driving around with a loaded gun in the car was not something I liked to do. I have no way of knowing whether his response was a veiled reference to a feud the Bustos and Marques families had conducted in the thirties and which climaxed when the Bustos men ambushed the Marques men, killing one of them outside the dance hall during the annual village fiesta, but in which the object of their attack, the locally notorious Johnny Marques, escaped and was never seen again. Two of the Bustos men were tried and convicted of murder, served their time, and then resumed their lives in the village, and I have always wondered whether Larry Bustos's paranoia was not connected to a fear transmitted from generation to generation of the day when Johnny Marques would come back to the valley to avenge a murder of fifty years before. Later, when Larry became *mayordomo,* he took to carrying a shotgun on his rounds out of a fear, he professed, of rattlesnakes. A short, stocky fellow, strong as an ox, Larry speaks in a slow, deliberate voice, deep and booming, and insists on finishing his sentences or speeches without interruption, as if they are coming out of him on tape. He speaks an Arabic-sounding Spanish with a heavy aspiration of the *jota,* (the Spanish *j,* pronounced like the English *h*), but his sometimes severe look and manner are mitigated by large, sensuous doe-eyes. As a commissioner I found him exasperating in the way *mayordomos* usually are to those attempting to supervise them, and our relations became just short of acrimonious during his two-year term, perhaps because I was not yet able to understand or fully know what happens to those who, at the age of twenty-five or so, assume the positions their fathers and grandfathers once held and so take

20

on the whole baggage of a past invisible to the outsider. Since then he has married and fathered a brood of boys, and time and work have done much to mellow him.

We are due for a break soon. Another section and we'll be almost to a house with an outdoor tap. Then comes a stretch where the bank is very low and needs to be built up. I want the crew to be fresh to dig *una pal' abajo* along there, the depth of a shovel blade. The *parciante* once kept horses and cows which wore the bank down over the years in climbing up to drink. Also it is sandy along there, the soil does not support the rich growth of those places where the ages have shifted loads of clay from the hillside down toward the valley.

My long *tareas* have carried us further than I expected. "*Y diecisiete*. After this one, take a break." Used to be, several years ago, they would call out "Chupin' time" for a break, from *chupar,* to suck, smoke. We stop for breaks usually where there is water, back of a house. "*¡Agua!*" I shout after a moment, prolonging the vowels. The *piones* know I won't inspect this section. The younger boys bound away across a field where apple trees were uprooted a couple of years ago by an irascible absentee landowner, a logger in the Northeast who has become intolerant of standing trees. The hulks of his apple trees, their bark dark red, now lie prone amid dry grass. The boys vault over and crawl under a fence toward a grey mobile home set amid its own apple trees freshly pruned. Nests of plum-colored prunings litter the ground. The more lethargic workers follow the ditch course around a bend and climb up on the low bank and drop down into the back yard and walk past an empty pig pen. Discreetly, behind the garage, the teenagers will gather to pass a joint, if they have not already done so before starting work. Dope makes them quiet, methodical workers, docile. I walk along the ditch to a sunny spot and sit down with the old men, next to Reynaldo Vasques. He and Orlando Serrano and Ewaldo Serrano chatter away lazily, fitfully in Spanish, switching to English briefly as I sit. A beautiful sunny morning. Still no wind. Nothing much to say. Stare into the hazy warming light of the morning. Bask. The two smokers roll their Prince Albert and light up.

I awake to the fact that I am the only gringo on the crew this morning. My son and one of his schoolmates have gone skiing, and the other Anglo kid who worked yesterday has gone to a better-paying job in Santa Fe. I used to worry about playing the part of the Boss, the Man. No longer. I have worked to become a neighbor. In winter I tend to spend time with Anglos, but in summer I am more likely to work with my Hispanic neighbors, an alternation which has become as natural to me as staying indoors in winter, working outside in summer. I am less certain of who I am—but less troubled by the lack of certainty. It depends on when, where, with whom. Here, sitting on a ditch bank and wondering what plant the star-shaped cluster of small green leaves peeping out of the dry grass might be, I am *mayordomo* of a very small irrigation ditch. My position would be a curiosity to most people I take pleasure in conversing with in the city and would be to them probably of little more importance than the identity of the plant emerging at my feet. "Is it good for anything?" What good is it to be the *mayordomo* of the Acequia de la Jara? Very little. Possibly none. My salary is one hundred dollars a month for six or seven months. What was once a position given to a respected elder in the old days—if there were old days, and perhaps these are still the old days here—is now foisted onto the old, the stay-at-homes, sometimes even the derelicts, or is occasionally coveted only by desperate young men in their early twenties who see in the modest salary the illusion, a road—somehow—to freedom and self-respect, an escape from the confines of this narrow valley. A job nobody much wants. But nonetheless a job, one of the few that a small community can give, often reluctantly, to one of its members. No, by becoming *mayordomo* you do not become the Man, even if you are a gringo. You become something quite opposite. You become even more involved and entwined. Next to blood relationships, which rule the valley, come water relationshps. The arteries of ditches and bloodlines cut across each other in patterns of as-

23

tounding complexity. Some families own properties on two or three of the valley's nine ditches. You can argue that the character of a man or woman can be as much formed by genetic and cultural material as by the location of their garden or chile patch along the length of a ditch, toward the beginning where water is plentiful or at the tail end where it will always be fitful and scarce. "He's that way because he lives at the bottom of the ditch and never gets any water" is an accepted explanation for even the most aberrant behavior in this valley. The man who lives at the bottom of a ditch is forever expectant, forever disappointed. My number *catorce,* Reynaldo Vasques, lives at the bottom of our ditch, the penultimate *parciante.* He has reason to distrust every one of the twenty-some *parciantes* above him. Age has given him a certain tolerance of his fate, but over the years he and his family have threatened lawsuits against upstream *parciantes*—including myself on one occasion—over water, and his sons have pulled guns on neighbors over water and women. We get along now, I have learned how to grow chile from him, he trades me chile seed for garlic, and I understand his position of being one who has always lived at the bottom of the ditch, at the end of the line, as did his parents and grandparents. Two or three times a year, first as commissioner and now as *mayordomo,* I take the precaution of telling him to telephone me when the water starts getting scarce down at his place. "Don't wait until the last minute when your chile is wilting and then get angry at everyone for not letting you have any water." But old habits die hard. He still waits for the last minute. "I haven't had any water for five days," comes his scratchy voice quavering over the *days,* "five days," he will repeat out the open pickup window on a morning search up and down the ditch for who's taking all the water. But he no longer gets angry at me. He knows I'll get the water down to him in a few hours. I'll call up the habitual water hogs—the two or three *parciantes* who leave their ditch gates open all day and night for weeks on end—and tell them to close their gates and let the water go past. Or drive around, as Reynaldo used to do when he was *mayordomo,* and close them myself. As *mayordomo* you become the pump, the heart that moves the vital fluid down the artery to the little plots of land of each of the cells, the *parciantes*. Water relationships would be simple and linear were they not complicated by all those other ways that human beings are connected with and divided from each other: blood, race, religion, education, politics, money. Against human constrictions and diversions the *mayordomo* must pump water seven months of the year. You can even come to envy those who work far away from here in institutions which deal with human beings piecemeal, one category at a time, and have thus managed to subordinate or exclude concerns peripheral to their specialized central purpose or to consign them to some vague world out beyond the parking lot. A *mayordomo* has to deal with people whole, often angry, in their own backyards, on their own property, regarding a commonplace substance that can inspire passion like no other, with all connections everywhere firmly in place, including who beat up on who twenty years before in the village school yard.

Water. The crew straggles back through the newly pruned apple trees, across the thick brown orchard grass, and climbs up the ditch bank, wiping away the last traces of water from their mouths with sleeves and wrists.

Agua.

"*¡Uno!*" My *número uno* has got lost somewhere, as has *número dos.* In a mock-shouting voice I call out the first numbers as if I am marking off their *tareas.* In a moment I see the black hair and blue jacket of *número uno,* Ricky Santiago, as he scrambles back through the line of waiting men and followed by his companion, Sam Castillo. They must have thought we did this section. Ricky takes his position while *número dos* jumps down into the ditch. "*Uno,*" I call out more softly and then take the second of my two paces for his *tarea* and scratch a line across the sand with the pole. "*Dos hasta al cerco,*" number two up to the fence. I climb over the wire. "Along here *una pal' abajo.* We gotta build up this bank." I jump down into the ditch. "*Tres.*" This will be a beginning at least. If we dig a little extra along here over the course of two or three years, we will have a good bank built up. Only about half the crew, up to about number ten, need dig deep; beyond that the bank is high enough. "Clean the edges along here. *Y diecisiete.*"

The next property has high swelling banks from which sprout thick clumps of willow and poison oak, and the work is mainly cleaning out grass growing in the channel and piles of dead leaves that have fallen in. We move along quickly. This is another place in the valley where the deposits of clay have shifted from the hillside into the bottomland, creating a soil deep and rich. I rent the lower fields from the owners who live above the ditch in a remodeled adobe house with sharply pitched roofs, Don and Penelope Thompson. She is a potter of considerable regional reputation, while he has worked at Los Alamos for a number of years servicing electronic equipment; behind a fence in the backyard lie the gleanings of many years of patronizing the National Laboratory salvage yard, including a World War II searchlight. I grow garlic, gourds, corn, and chile in their lower fields, probably in violation of a state law I have heard about and which specifies that the *mayordomo* must not lease land on a ditch he is in charge of. Ours is a very small ditch, however, with small parcels of land, none larger than about eight acres, and you may argue that the spirit of the law seeks to prevent a *mayordomo* from favoring his own land over that of other *parciantes*. Whether he owns his own land, leases or rents it does not much alter the problem, unless in fact he controls a significant portion of the land on the ditch, thereby creating a situation in which he could in effect elect himself— though this would depend on whether *parciantes* vote by shares or by membership. (The Acequia de la Jara has always voted by membership in my time, one vote per *parciante*.) As long as the *mayordomo* is a landowner, which serves to guarantee that he will take a proprietary interest in the flow of water, there will always be a degree of conflict of interest, particularly in a very small organization, just as there will almost always be some nepotism and favoritism. And there will always be an element of self-interest in my involvement in the ditch, given the fact that I depend on its water for much of my living. I depend very much on the labor of this crew to clean the ditch that will deliver water to my two fields. In turn, the crew, or rather the *parciantes* paying most of them, depend on my labor as *mayordomo* to deliver water to their fields. The law reminds me to be fair, not to take advantage of my position or more advantage than it inherently gives me.

We move rapidly into the next place, which belongs to a commissioner of the ditch, Ignacio Serna, whose main work is to countersign my monthly paycheck. He is a janitor at a school district fifty miles away and leaves for work in the middle of the afternoon, returning home at one in the morning five days a week. His bosses and the teachers whose classrooms he cleans are mostly Anglos, and I think it must give him secret pleasure to sign the paycheck of a man who has a college education, which he does with a little flourish preceded by an uncertain "Here?" before bringing the pen down to the signature line on the check spread out on the hood of my truck. Every now and then in the past, resentments would swell up and burst out into weekends of drinking, and he would place rocks across the dirt road past his house or drive down to my place and complain about kids on bicycles disturbing his dogs, and he is often still a little drunk and outspoken at the annual ditch meetings—such behavior followed, a day or two later, by profuse apologies and ingratiating smiles and laughs. During summer work crews he often displays the morbid humor of Lear's Fool, and once he proposed that we bury the then *mayordomo,* Paco Ortiz, in the ditch bank, in order to strengthen it. I am fond of Ignacio (except when he's very drunk), and I think he trusts me as someone who might be a friend and who perhaps knows that being elected ditch commissioner once a year may be his one honor in a life of swabbing floors and emptying wastebaskets.

It is just past eleven-thirty. The high banks have been eaten clean of vegetation along here by generations of Ignacio Serna's sheep and goats and chickens and pigs, though this year nothing stirs in the ramshackle pens along the lower side of the ditch except a few barred-rock hens and a pair of sheep in a cramped wire coop. The next section encompasses a siphon under an arroyo and a culvert that passes beneath the highway. This means breaking the crew into three groups and foregoing inspection. I decide to dismiss them early for lunch. Not all the men and boys have cars or can get rides to their houses a mile or more away: a few must always walk.

"Break for lunch," I call out. "Be back here at one." I stash my pole, *la vara,* in the bushes where we are to resume.

"*Lonche,*" voices echo. Sound of V-8 engines roaring to life, gravel splashing, clatter of shovels landing in the back of pickups, over the growl of a Diesel backhoe backfilling the walls of a cement-block root cellar one of Ignacio Serna's sons has built next to the house. I set off on foot down the dirt road toward home, a quarter of a mile downriver, back down the way we have been working all morning.

Two

La Junta Valley (as I have called it), nestled like a slightly folded leaf within the foothills of the Sangre de Cristo Range, is some three miles long and from a quarter- to a half-mile wide, with the Rio de la Junta flowing east to west back and forth across its central axis in a meandering course. Four of the *acequias* water fields to the north of the river, five to the south, where the majority of the five to seven hundred inhabitants live, perhaps seven-eighths of them Hispanic descendants of eighteenth-century colonists and the remnants of a nearby Pueblo Indian settlement, the remainder Anglos who have settled in the valley over the past twenty years. The Rio de la Junta flows out of the western end of the valley and eventually into the Rio Grande; at the same end, a two-lane highway connects the valley to the cities to the south and the mountain communities to the east and north. The highway passes through the center of the village of La Junta, with its post office, general store, elementary school, Catholic and Presbyterian churches, and Texaco station, on the high ground south of the river. A mile and a half east of the village center, the highway crosses the Rio de la Junta on a low concrete bridge, built in the mid-1950s, and then heads straight uphill, north, toward the foothills of the Sangre de Cristos, up a long arroyo which runs parallel to the highway on the west and drains into the river from the north. This arroyo, the Cañada de Cobre, runs perhaps three or four times a year at most; some years it never runs at all, or with no more than a muddy trickle following a downpour. But a thundershower in summer, if heavy and prolonged enough, can send a temporary river of reeking muddy water a foot or more deep and thirty feet wide down the sandy rock-strewn course for two or three hours, cutting an impassable furrow across the dirt road that connects the houses and fields of the uppermost dozen *parciantes* of the Acequia de la Jara to the highway. When the highway department put in the concrete bridge thirty years ago, it rerouted the arroyo to the west, moving it downriver, and installed a three-foot-diameter siphon in the shape of a spreadout U under the arroyo bed, to allow passage of the water of the Acequia de la Jara. The siphon is about forty feet long. In the years I have worked with the ditch the siphon has become plugged up only once—but cleared

itself after half an hour. I have long thought we ought
to install some sort of grate to keep brush, trash, and
rocks from washing into it, and also to prevent small
children from falling in. From the mouth of the siphon the ditch course runs upstream thirty feet or so
before passing through a straight culvert under the
highway and then another twenty feet to a point
where the end of the Acequia de los Cerritos passes
over our ditch via another short culvert, toward the
small triangular chile patch of its last *parciante* and
from there back to the river. When we are unable to
get enough water down our ditch from the dam, for
one reason or another, we ask the Acequia de los Cerritos if we can divert their tailwater to our ditch, a
matter of shoveling out a narrow channel in the turf
and blocking the mouth of their culvert. Protocol re-
quires commissioners to negotiate this minor matter,
but in fact it is most often the two *mayordomos* who
actually do so, while agreeing to ask their commissions about it sooner or later.

A ditch's tailwater—water left over at the end of the
ditch—is supposed to go back into the river so that
the next ditches down the line will have enough to fill
their channels. So goes the popular reasoning. Our
river, however, has two sources of flow. The first
seven ditches at the top or eastern end of the valley
obtain their water directly from mountain runoff, or
whatever is left over from the high valleys that lie between us and the forests, and when we have a dry year

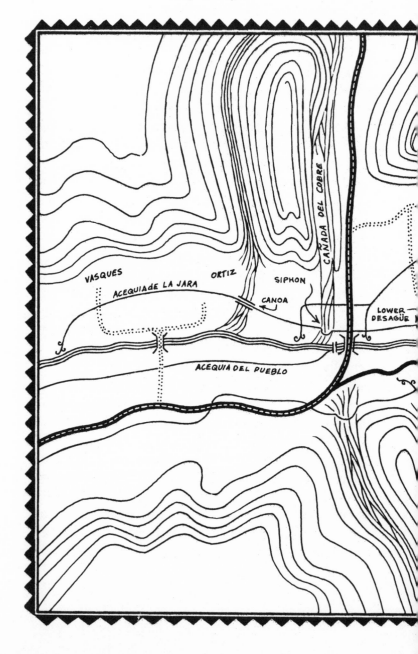

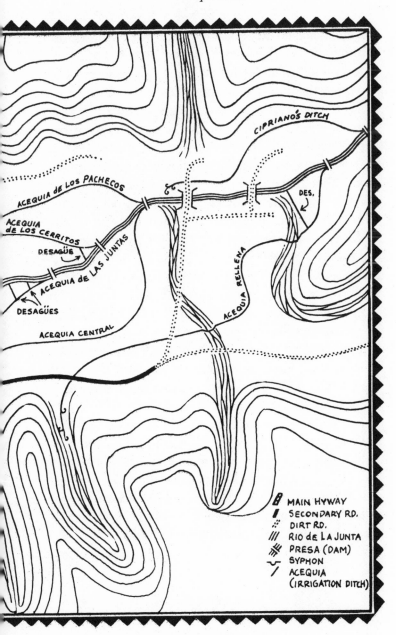

CIPRIANO'S DITCH

ACEQUIA DE LOS PACHECOS

ACEQUIA DE LOS CERRITOS

DESAGÜE

ACEQUIA DE LAS JUNTAS

DESAGÜES

ACEQUIA CENTRAL

ACEQUIA RELLENA

DES.

MAIN HYWAY	
SECONDARY RD.	
DIRT RD.	
RIO DE LA JUNTA	
PRESA (DAM)	
SYPHON	
ACEQUIA (IRRIGATION DITCH)	

the most heated negotiations take place among the commissions of these seven upper ditches about procedures and schedules for dividing up the river. The two lowermost ditches in the valley are fed by springs when the river otherwise dries up—which is to say that our ditch, whose dam is the lowermost of the upper seven, will take the very last of the flow from the river, while a quarter of a mile below, at the highway crossing, there will be enough water in the river again to serve the needs of the Acequia del Pueblo, whose diversion dam lies immediately west of the highway bridge. Springs replenish the river again several hundred yards below the highway, in turn eventually feeding the very last ditch whose dam is at the westernmost end of the valley just before the gap. On the whole, springs, though no doubt fed in large part by the ditches themselves, are probably more important than tailwater for keeping the river flowing in dry seasons, and one may argue that much of the water used in the valley eventually leaves it again with relatively little diminishment.

The traveler crossing the highway bridge at fifty miles an hour will not see a river so much as a desperately small trickle of water feeling its way through a bed of bone-white rocks much of the year; and the out-of-towner, in general, is not likely to notice most of the ditch works through this important stretch— the siphon and culvert of our ditch and that of the Acequia de los Cerritos, the two siphons of the Ace-

quia de las Juntas across the river, one under an arroyo
and the other under the highway itself, works which
are all inconspicuous in comparison with the gran-
diose riprap and concrete construction of the *presa,*
the dam, of the Acequia del Pueblo, just downriver
from the highway bridge. It is a peculiar structure apparently designed to protect the headgates from the
pounding effects of the Cañada de Cobre in full flood
as it enters the river channel immediately opposite,
more than to actually direct the normal flow of river
water toward the gates, which the galleried highway
bridge tends to do anyway. The dam is an almost ma-
rine construction and suggests a dry dock or break-
water (which in fact it is) or canal lock misconstructed
in the middle of what is, at times, an almost nonexis-
tent stream.

At a quarter of one I drive my pickup from the
house up to the dirt road to the highway and park it at
the stop sign opposite the entrance to our siphon.
Unless a wind comes up, which seems unlikely given
the continued haziness of the sky, the afternoon will
be pleasantly warm. In two hours and without working too hard we should be able to finish digging the
ditch from here to the lower *desagüe,* or sluice gate.
For several years we have been unable to shut off the
ditch between the lower and upper *desagües* for lack of
a proper headgate at the dam. No amount of ply-
wood, plastic, or old carpeting seems to stop com-

pletely the flow of water through a short section of culvert three feet in diameter at the pondlike upper *desagüe,* with the result that there is a half-mile stretch of ditch where the water runs all year round. We have only one *parciante* along there, Rupert Castillo, down from two when the second, José Castillo, lost his small parcel of land to floodwaters about ten years ago. The ditch parallels the river at the lower or southern end of orchards and pastureland served for the most part by the Acequia de los Cerritos from the high ground to the north, and it is in the interest of some of the Cerritos landowners to see our ditch running all winter long through the lower end of their fields to provide water for their cows. This spring I gave up trying to shut off the upper *desagüe* after several years of failing at it. I suspect José Castillo of having helped to undo my work. I have often seen him working his way along the river and ditch banks with a gunny sack and sickle and wearing a stained felt hat, cutting alfalfa for his pigs and chickens from May onward. His house sits up on the hillside of the hamlet of Los Cerritos overlooking the long narrow field where he keeps his cows and which ends in our ditch—and where they drink all year round. I imagine José Castillo takes perverse pleasure in watching me park my truck just below his house in the early spring and in observing me hike down through Harold Castillo's apple orchard toward the ditch two hundred yards below, shovel and sheets of black plastic in hand; sitting on his porch, he will imagine me trying to plug up the mouth of the *desagüe* culvert once again a week or two before we are scheduled to dig out the ditch. (The main function of the culvert is to protect the ditch from surging water during a flood by restricting the amount of water that can flow into the ditch proper.) He will watch me trudge back up through the orchard, climb back into my truck, turn around in Harold Castillo's driveway, drive away; then, in an hour or so, perhaps even the next morning or the day after, he will walk down to check on his cows and will climb the fence and follow the ditch bank up to the culvert where a few cuts in the plastic, a tug at it, will set the ditch to running again for his cows— and he knows I will not trouble to come back day after day to try to stop it up again. This is what, perhaps unfairly, I imagine him doing. He is a stoop-shouldered man in his sixties with a long and somewhat twisted face and a round teeth-baring mouth, which can sometimes smile stiffly, and large liquid brown eyes. He seems to know little English, but even his utterances in Spanish are limited to a few words grunted from the depths of his chest. He is the father of Johnny Castillo, my shovel-banging tormentor of fifteen years ago.

The workers begin arriving. I know all their names now and can check them off the list without asking who they are. They park their cars and trucks along the highway and the dirt road, and a few drive down to Ignacio Serna's place and leave them there inside his fence. The first *vuelta* is going to be messy because I'll have to assign three workers to the section before the siphon, another three or four in the short section between the siphon and the highway culvert, and the rest across the highway. But none of these places needs to be dug out very well. Everyone arrives on time this afternoon, and we start out punctually at one.

The highway marks the border between the territories, as it were, of the Acequia de la Jara and the Acequia de los Cerritos and their respective communities. Across the highway the ditch bank forms a border to the very well-kept lawn and apple orchard of the Leandro Castillo place through which our ditch passes, as it angles toward the river, but does not serve. I order some overzealous *piones* to put out a fire they have ignited in the long dry grass growing down into the channel. "Shovel your dirt over on this bank, on the river side," I tell the crew, so we won't mess up Leandro Castillo's lawn on the other side. This "by law" we don't have to do, we can put the dirt on either bank we want, but I prefer to stay on the good side of Leandro, who will otherwise take to telephoning me whenever the ditch runs high and threatens to flood his lawn and, he claims, make his septic tank back up. I suspect that the ditch channel tends to sink or settle along this sandy stretch as every year we dig out large amounts of fine silt. I walk along the grass with my pole. "Just clean the edges."

But they are all digging their heads off. Well, let them: it will raise the bank. Then I see that my *números uno* and *dos,* Ricky Santiago and Sam Castillo, have finished their *tareas* and have walked down to the tail end of the line to mark off their next *tareas* themselves, next to *diecisiete,* and have begun to dig them out. Ricky Santiago is a tall, skinny fellow of sixteen or so, very polite yet also somewhat closed. He is one of two kids on the crew today whose fathers were killed in car wrecks; he lives with his mother and stepfather, both office workers, in a mobile home on the other side of the valley. He's the kind of "nice kid" who finds himself in frequent minor scrapes, is probably bright enough for college but who may at best end up in the service. Though I approve of his trying to get ahead, in this case it makes it difficult for me to inspect his *tarea.* I amble over to him and his partner in upward mobility. "I appreciate your enthusiasm but I would like you to stay in your *tareas,* both of you, until everybody's ready to move." Neither of them argues.

Two *vueltas* move us to the fence at the edge of the lawn where Leandro has cut down some cottonwood trees over his pigpen but without bothering to clear the shattered branches out of the ditch. The pigpen is empty this year. After the fence the ditch runs along the edge of the river for perhaps a quarter of a mile through cottonwoods and junipers to the lower *desagüe;* with the fragrant junipers and the sound of the water in the river thirty feet below, this is a pleasant and graceful stretch. Another *vuelta* and we are in the shade. The afternoon is warm. The effects of lunch are making everyone lethargic. I call a break. The older men find a shady bank and sit down facing the river below. They chatter away softly in Spanish. I sit down next to Reynaldo. They are all talking about their service days. *La Alemania. El Japón. Corea.* Reynaldo turns to me and asks in English: "Were you in the service?" "No. I stayed in college. And there was a family friend on the draft board." And the doctor who presided over my birth also helped, exaggerating my childhood asthma. And there were other reasons I never had to go, coming as I did from an area in California where there were numerous military bases and a ready supply of service-family recruits. I was too young for Korea, too old or clever for Vietnam. "Many people went from here," Reynaldo observes, almost scolding. He adds that nobody went to college then, except a couple of men and women who became the village schoolteachers. Growing up in a backwoods village in New Mexico you don't learn how to get out of the draft. A lot of New Mexicans were in Bataan. Korea took its toll. A local boy was killed in Vietnam, posthumously awarded the Medal of Honor. I wonder at the effects on a small community stripped of its young men generation after generation. How many have been killed in those three wars? So many? As many as the number who have died in car and motorcycle and shooting and drowning accidents over the years, even since I have been here? What, I wonder, has been the enormous toll of alcohol?

The conversation slips back into Spanish. I have never become fluent in the local variant. I speak Spanish when I can—counting the numbers for the *vueltas,* making little observations, but less to show my linguistic talents than to suggest that Spanish is the proper language of the ditch. I am somewhat like a person who grows up in the household of the language of the old country and who can understand much of what is spoken around him while yet unable to speak more than a few words himself. Many young Chicanos, particularly those not raised with their grandparents, are in much the same position. English now has the right of way here, and very few local people will persist in speaking Spanish if you show signs of having difficulty: they will switch to English if they speak it, as the vast majority now do, or else fall silent. Through centuries of relative isolation, the local Spanish of northern New Mexico has become an archaic variant, sometimes angry and depressed, so to speak, even bitter, lacking in confidence, something of an argot, an almost secret language hiding out in the hills where it knows it will never reconquer the cities: dying yet still alive. And paradoxically more alive in its way, I sometimes think, than much media-blitzed English with its tenuous connections to experienced realities and its infestations of that cultural wisdom we now call "information." This has

not been a ditch cleaning, today and the two days before, when the local Spanish has joked and sung and
punned away the hours and made the digging time
wing by in laughter and shouting, but I have been
with crews like that in the past. My crew has been
relatively quiet this year: their silences may be the
sound of a language dying. The *acequia* may be the
dialect's last defense position, the final trench, the
place where annually it most loudly celebrates itself.
My persistent presence here—the traditional enemy—
is perhaps a sign of dissolution. Anglos who go off to
Mexico or Spain and who come back speaking "good"
or "proper" Castilian Spanish threaten the local dialect from yet another direction—while others, the
fashionable developers in Santa Fe and Taos, pay lip
service to it by giving Spanish names to their streets
and businesses and subdivisions. I grew up in a sub-
urb in Southern California where the towns and
streets all had Spanish names but no Hispanic inhabitants—other than the Mexican nationals who slipped
across the border and who wandered the suburbs in
search of yard work. As time passes the real-estate
Spanish of Santa Fe and its new suburbs may be all
that survives of the colorful variants of the villages of
northern New Mexico—like the old Santa Fe *acequias*
which no longer carry water but which are now and
then still cleaned out for their historic interest or curiosity value.

This has been a long break. We have perhaps three more *vueltas* to go. They will carry us to the lower *desagüe* around two-thirty. It is almost two now. I realize I had better start filling out the *papelitos,* the chits, for the workers. But first I'll assign them their *tareas.* "*Vámonos.* Let's go." The ditch passes back under a fence here, into the lower end of a large pasture which drains its excess water from the Acequia de los Cerritos into our channel. There used to be a spot along here with a short section of culvert where the bank had been broken down on the river side by the combined work of cows and muskrats. Last year we dug out the culvert, which had rusted through, and lined the bank with plastic and built it up. It still leaks somewhere along here but not as badly as before. "Build up the bank along here," I call out as I mark off the *tareas.* At the end of the *vuelta* the ditch passes back under the fence. I climb over and find a shady spot to fill out the *papelitos.* I'll credit the workers with six hours for the five they will have actually worked. *Papelitos* are three-by-five Xeroxed forms which the *mayordomo* is to fill out, noting the date, number of hours worked, amount to be paid, the name of the worker, the type of work, and the *parciante* in whose name the work has been performed. The *papelito* is given to the worker at the end of the day; the worker then takes it to his *parciante* for payment. The lucky *pión* will be paid in cash, the unlucky one with a personal check he will have to cash at the local store or bar—or worse, if he is unable to find his *parciante* after a reasonable time, six in the evening or so, or if the *parciante* finds himself broke at that particular moment, then the *pión* with his still unnegotiated chit can go to the ditch treasurer and ask for a check from the ditch itself, a check that will require a counter signature by a second commissioner. By then, or course, the store will have closed and the bar owner will be fed up with underage kids coming to cash checks. Today I have alerted the treasurer to the possibility that a couple of *piones* might show up with their *papelitos,* so there should be checks ready with both signatures on them. There are also kids who get their checks but for some reason—timidity? affluence?—don't cash them for a month or two and carry them around in their wallets so that when they finally come back from the bank they are all creased and tattered, with tiny slanted signatures on the backs.

Parciantes who work for themselves do not get *papelitos* unless they ask for them as proof that they have put in their time on the ditch cleaning, perhaps not trusting the accuracy of my daily roll sheets, which are what I fill out the *papelitos* from. The roll-call sheet, once I go over it for errors, eventually ends up in the treasurer's records; the treasurer uses it to enter information on to the *parciantes'* account sheets as either work performed (*trabajo*) or as delinquent hours converted into money at the rate of $2.50 an hour (*de-*

lincuencias) to be collected from the *parciante* at a later date. These can be somewhat confusing calculations— six hours' *delincuencias* for a *parciante* with one and three-quarters *piones* (meaning shares in this use), for example—but I discovered in my years as treasurer that if you keep the work crew records in good order, most errors and claims can be easily straightened out. A common situation is that a *parciante* will go to the treasurer a year or two afterward and say, "But I sent Pete López for eight hours that Saturday three years ago, but my wife can't find the *papelito*," and the treasurer can look up the work crew record for that particular day and find out that Pete only worked two hours that morning like everybody else on the crew, not a full day. The forms for the individual account sheets, the daily work-crew roll-call sheets, and the *papelitos*—all of these I designed myself some years back after discovering the weaknesses of paperwork improvised anew each spring; also I instituted what I hope will remain the custom of once a year Xeroxing and mailing to all *parciantes* copies of their individual account sheets in order to establish a basis for reconstructing ditch records should the master file be lost or destroyed.

I mark off the next *tareas* without inspecting the last *vuelta*. The ditch banks are high along here and in good condition; there is no need for more than a superficial cleaning. A fat cottonwood leans over the channel at the last *tarea*. Between it and the lower *de-*

sagüe there are about three *tareas,* or twenty-five feet, left over. A trickle of water is running into the *desagüe,* a low crumbling cement box with splashboard gates opening into the ditch in one direction and back toward the river in another. The *desagüe* serves as the final regulating point for the water that will flow into the mile-long section of the ditch we are about to finish cleaning. Surplus water is diverted back into the river via two outlets, the first a low wall of loose stones designed to break down in the event of a flooding surge of water coming down from the upper *desagüe* and the dam, and the second a short cement channel that is now open but that can be blocked by two or three wooden splashboards dropped into slots in the cement walls. A similar, though wider, wooden gate now blocks the channel into the ditch; this can be raised by a series of notches to regulate in a rough manner the amount of water flowing into the ditch or can be lowered completely, as it is now, and sealed with dirt and clumps of grass. The cement works of the small structure, which is about the size of two bathtubs, are crumbling badly and it is impossible to block the water completely in any direction, so to be certain that we won't have water leaking down the ditch just before cleaning time, as used to happen now and then, I have taken to blocking the ditch channel with a foot-high berm of sand shoveled down from the bank midway between the *desagüe* and the leaning cottonwood. Almost anything can make the

desagüe plug up and cause the water to flow in unexpected directions here, including blowing tumbleweeds in the spring and branches floating down from
the dam during floods; but since I started putting in
the berm no water has entered the main channel before the cleaning, and we haven't had to deal with trying to dig out a muddy or frozen mess. I come here
once a week or so during the irrigation season to
clean out debris caught under the splashboards and to
regulate the water, and if the flow is too high or low
coming into the *desagüe* I know there is a problem up
at the dam, which is more difficult to get to. This is
also where I come to shut off the water during an
emergency. I have suggested to the commission that
eventually we abandon this *desagüe* and build a new
one at the highway, where the Acequia de los Cerritos
crosses over our ditch, a location that is far more accessible. The old *desagüe* is also constructed in such a
manner that it fails to do what every *desagüe* should
do, which is to sluice silt and debris back into the
river; instead it does quite the opposite, sending silt
and trash on down into the main ditch channel. Yet I
am fond of this wooded spot and its crumbling construction, a place where I come to divide the waters
into what we'll use and what we'll turn noisily back
to the river, a place where the water comes swirling
around a bend down from the dam and passes under a
fence to surge chirping into the cement channel, half
of it to splash over a weathered pine two-by-six back

to the river, the rest to slip under the gate and glide smoothly, composed again, unruffled, under the cottonwood tree and pass out of sight around a leaning fence overgrown with creeper, toward our orchards and fields. As a child this is the sort of spot I would seek out to play in, to watch the water, note how things floated and drifted and sank, await the appearance of small creatures in the algae-grown depths.

I walk back down the line, around the cottonwood tree, back to the beginning. "We've got three more *tareas* to do up there and then we'll be finished." I beckon to numbers *uno, dos,* and *tres*. Everyone is in a good mood now, laughing as the four of us walk back up the line. The work is nearly over. It hasn't been bad. I have been on crews where the workers have been sorry to see it all finish at the end of the cleaning: something to do, someone to talk to, old acquaintances renewed, work without complications amid friends and neighbors, some spending money. The three workers quickly remove the sand berm across the channel and clean up the rest of their *tareas*. The crew, the young ones, crowd around me as I pull the *papelitos* from a pocket. "Clyde. Where are you? Roberto. Tim, do you know where these people live?" He doesn't, so I start giving him directions but his friend says he knows where. "Sammy, did they pay you yesterday?" Yes, they did and they said they would pay him today as well. "Rudy, if you have a problem with this one take the *papelito* to the treasurer." And so on down the line, all fifteen or so I have written up *papelitos* for. I watch them fan out across the alfalfa field, loping across a shortcut back toward the highway and their cars and trucks, shovels shiny with work and flashing in the sunlight, the crew becoming now the diaspora of what the past two days had welded itself into a collective creature, an animal of sorts, a large denim-clad caterpillar, moody and good humored, defiant and somnolent by alternations, but in all a good worker this year. The older men walk more slowly together down the winding ditch channel. I catch up with Ricardo Serna and ask him if he could help bring the water down Monday afternoon. In his forties, Ricardo's out of work and I know he's always interested in making a few bucks for part of an afternoon. "Sure. What time?"

I ask him to be at my place at one. But we'll need a chainsaw and neither of us has one. The ditch channel between the two *desagües* is badly clogged with brush, and beavers have been felling trees all winter near the dam; perhaps there will be work for three of us. Back down at the highway I flag down Orlando Serrano. He is a big shambling man, now retired from mine work in Nevada, and during his many years away from the valley he piled up several hundred dollars in *delincuencias* on his property, which I have let him work off since his return. He still owes some money. Yes, he can come Monday afternoon. "*¿Puede traer la serruche?*" "*Sí,*" he nods.

I climb in my truck and drive slowly down the dirt road the quarter of a mile back to the house. For a few hours this afternoon there will be an increase in traffic up and down the driveways of this side of the river as my workers search out their *parciantes* to be paid. Today's Saturday, which means everybody will be in town shopping, but they will be home a little earlier than weekdays, when they are at work. When I get home I lift the cottonwood pole out of the back of the truck, the one I used to mark off the *tareas, la vara,* and lean it in the corner of the adobe wall next to the front door, where it will stay until next March when the Acequia de la Jara will be cleaned once again— for perhaps the seventieth or hundredth or two-hundredth time.

Three

If you were to climb the hillside out of the Junta Valley to the top of the mesa or to various hilltops or prominences to the north you would look back down on a narrow, slightly curving valley two or three miles long and divided not quite down the middle by a fringe of silver-branched cottonwoods that line a glinting ribbon of water also bordered in winter by strips of snow. The Rio de la Junta meanders back and forth through the valley east to west, its course having been pushed this way and that over the millennia by repeated dumpings of sand and gravel from ten or so arroyos, and by the steepness and slowness of its own descent, which dictates where its loads of silt, sand, gravel, and even boulders and logs will be deposited or carried along in times of flood. Less pronounced files of cottonwood and willow and smoky thickets of wild plum here and there mark the watercourses of the nine irrigation ditches that run parallel to the river along the middle and high ground of the valley on both the north and south sides. At right angles to ditches and to the river run innumerable fencelines and hedgerows that divide up the arable land into hundreds of parcels a fourth of an acre to ten acres in size, and many of which are presided over by a tin-roof house or a bright new mobile home. From the west or lower end of the valley, to trace its route in the direction we cleaned it out Friday and Saturday, the twenty-second and twenty-third of March, 1985, the channel of the Acequia de la Jara follows a course at the base of the hillside to the north, separated from the river by two hundred yards of bottomland fields, up the valley a mile or so to the highway crossing at the river, where the channel angles southward over to the very edge of the river, which it then follows closely another half-mile to the point where it connects with it at the *presa,* the dam, yearly improvised anew out of rocks and brush. As you look down on the fields and orchards in late March where as yet no green will show from your prominence of two or three hundred feet above the valley floor, surveying the grey tin roofs glinting in the sun, the rusty tin roofs of the older adobe houses, you will hear the faint hiss of a car moving slowly along the distant highway in the moments the wind drops, or the birdlike jabbering of schoolchildren in the school yard during recess, a dog barking down below, sheep bleating to be fed, the crowing of roosters and the honking of geese—while from above, from a sky under which most things seem to cower in smallness so wide is the glare of its immense blueness, you will hear the rumble of a jet passing twenty thousand feet overhead, bound for Denver or Los Angeles, San Francisco, Chicago, or New York.

Down below on Monday afternoon, two days after the ditch cleaning, another fine clear day, Ricardo Serna walks up my drive at a quarter to one with a shovel, rousing the dogs from their daylong siesta. This is the day we will put water into the ditch, the twenty-fifth of March, and our ditch will be as usual the first in the valley to have water running in it. I throw my shovel along with his into the back of my pickup, also a rake and a pitchfork, and we drive up to the highway to await Orlando Serrano and his chainsaw at the stop sign. He arrives at the appointed hour and we pile our tools into the back of his high, green four-wheel-drive Ford pickup and climb in with him. To reach the dam you have to drive up the highway a quarter of a mile north and then turn right on to a dirt road through Los Cerritos, a village whose adobe houses are set close together at odd angles on the high ground above the north side of the valley, with a dramatic view of the snow-capped Sangre de Cristo Range to the east. I am reminded of Europe here, villages in Provence or on Crete, not so much by the tin roofs or the adobe walls but by the way the houses are built close to each other in a spectacular setting. Supposedly there are traces of Indian settlements up on the bluff to the north. The fields of Los Cerritos lie below to the right: pastures, apple orchards, newly plowed land for corn and chile patches, the *milpas* and the *huertas*. A half-mile through Los Cerritos on the winding narrow dirt road, here and there wide enough for two cars to pass, just below José Castillo's house up on the hillside with its rounded adobe *horno* made to look like a huge earthen head set in the ground with its open mouth (the oven door) and two eyes (the vent holes) peering out over the valley, I tell Orlando to pull over and park. He asks whether we can't drive down through Harold Castillo's orchard, but unfortunately I failed to ask him and don't like to drive down through there unless I check with Harold first. Orlando pulls the truck over onto the shoulder and we unload our tools, push through the steel footpath gate and cross a small steel bridge over the dry channel of the Acequia de los Cerritos, which runs along the edge of the road through here. Just inside the fence lies Harold's impressive scrap pile of huge culverts, catwalks, pipes, gates, and other pieces of steel acquired from the Los Alamos salvage yard. We set off down through the orchard toward the river. As long as you have a shovel in hand (or pitchfork or rake) local custom gives you the right to walk through anyone's property on ditch business. I consider Los Cerritos to be if not enemy territory then at least potentially hostile, and I make a point of keeping on friendly terms with the *mayordomo* of the Acequia de los Cerritos and particularly with a commissioner who lives two places up from our dam, of whom I am fond anyway, Alberto Manzanares. Between our dam and the highway, at which point Acequia de la Jara territory begins, you might say, our ditch crosses the bottomlands of perhaps a dozen properties through Los Cerritos, only one of which is served by our ditch. The walk always seems long down through Harold Castillo's apple orchard, across the roughly disked ground, perhaps a quarter of a mile, down to the cottonwoods that mark the end of his property and where our ditch channel splits off from the river course.

The area turns out to be a mess. At the *desagüe* beavers have cut down two large cottonwoods, felling them right across the water. We climb over the fence and survey the scene. Neither of the felled trees, both of them a foot and a half in diameter at the trunk, are actually in the water: one of them arches over the ditch channel, clearing the water, though the smaller branches droop into the flow and have collected a dam of floating debris. I give Orlando Serrano instructions to start blocking the ends of the tree but to leave the main trunk intact across the ditch. In the event of flooding this year, always likely, the log will serve to catch debris just as it is doing now and thus slow the surge of water into the main ditch channel. In the old days before concrete ditch gates—which we still do not have—you always placed a couple of logs across the mouth of the ditch at the dam just for this purpose. Modern times have not yet come to us except in the form of a short section of galvanized steel culvert three feet in diameter, which we dropped into the ditch channel several years ago with the idea that it would help us shut off the water into the ditch by giving us a firm structure against which to place boards and sheet plastic. The culvert is now clogged with debris—as in a sense it should be. The second felled cottonwood lies over it. I will ask Orlando to cut it in the same manner, block the ends but leave the main trunk intact. Both logs point toward the river and, being green and heavy, will serve in a flood to divert water back in that direction. With Orlando working away at the first tree, Ricardo and I walk up the ditch bank to the dam, such as it is. At best, in the middle of summer, the dam is a sweeping arc of piled up stones and branches curving out into the river to catch the water at a point where the river starts curving away from the north bank, a fragile structure reinforced by swaths of black plastic, old carpeting, and sheets of corrugated roofing salvaged from the dump, and held in place by the odd boulder deposited by a skip loader about ten years before. At least that was what it looked like in the fall when I was last down here. The river is running high now and much of the dam appears to have been washed away, but since the main force is directed more or less toward the mouth of the ditch, plenty of water is coming in. The main thing is to keep a good flow through the ditch channel between the dam, or where the dam is supposed to be, and the culvert at the upper *desagüe* so that the first hundred feet or so of the channel won't silt up on us. Ricardo and I move back down the ditch and set about pulling out a tangle of branches that have formed a small dam across the five-foot-wide channel halfway down to the *desagüe* and behind which silt and gravel are beginning to pile up. Dirty work this, on hands and knees, pulling and prying with pitchfork and rake, leaning over the water from a crumbling sandy bank.

By the time we have the obstruction cleared Orlando Serrano has blocked the ends of the cottonwood lying over the ditch and we can move down and begin pulling out the debris caught under it. Orlando handles his twenty-four-inch chainsaw like a toy, either courageous or foolhardy, I am uncertain which, ignoring all the safety rules in the book, the effect perhaps of a life working in the mines of Nevada. I suggest that he start cutting up the tree over the culvert. Ricardo and I set about fishing out a large collection of yellow willow twigs, beaver-chewed green and silver cottonwood branches, an assortment of worn and weathered roots and sticks washed perhaps all the way down from the high mountains over the course of a year or two, and in the greyish foam and brown grime of dead juniper needles, a sealed beam headlamp made in Japan. After snapping off the snagging twigs on the underside of the cottonwood log, we finish our work by pulling out a long submerged branch I pried up with the pitchfork to bring within reach. The water is now free to flow the fifteen feet or so to the culvert, which serves to limit what can then flow into the ditch proper beyond. The surplus water goes out the *desagüe:* that is, it flows over and under an overgrown wall of logs draped with the rotting remains of an old shag carpet Orlando Serrano presented to us a couple of years ago for this purpose. This informal structure is what we call the upper *desagüe.*

I direct Orlando upriver toward the dam to lop off the end of a fallen tree that is dragging in the water, while Ricardo and I unplug the culvert. I suspect a beaver or muskrat has decided this might be a good place to establish residence. Ricardo says he saw something in the water up here two weeks ago when we were cutting willows. Twig by twig we unplug the culvert until it belches forth a bolus of small branches and a sodden tumbleweed. While Orlando Serrano is finishing his work up at the dam, we fish a few of the larger branches out of the *desagüe* channel back to the river so the water won't dam up there and force too much down the ditch either through the culvert or over the top of the low bank of earth with which it is covered.

Mayordomo

Now we can begin following the water down. There
are more small dams of branches with silt building up
behind them the next hundred yards or so, a straight
and almost level run where the water flows sluggishly.
We pull and pry branches out with the pitchfork and
rake. Ricardo fishes out a headlamp. "Here's the other
one," he says. Even in nature they come in pairs. Orlando catches up with us. I tell him I'll credit him ten
dollars for chainsaw work, plus his time. Ricardo and
I can follow the water down on foot to the highway
by ourselves now, and I thank Orlando for his help
and send him on home, a decision I soon regret. The
work becomes grueling the next hundred yards as we
fish branches out of the ditch, along with boards,
sodden logs, tumbleweeds. The channel drops very
gradually along here, all the more reason to keep it
clear, though over the years it has eroded deeper and
deeper toward a the point where it begins to drop
more rapidly at the property owned by our sole *parciante* between the dam and the highway. The channel
is almost four feet deep here. To fish things out we
have to get down on hands and knees, bend over, hope
we don't fall in. Soon we are both panting and sweat-
ing. Then there are the fences to climb over or under
or through every twenty yards or so, plus the abandoned fences to avoid tripping over, fallen branches,
gopher holes; and we have also brought too many
shovels and have too much to carry. My new leather

gloves have gotten soaked, turning my hands a bright orange from the dye. At José Castillo's place, Ricardo tugs at a branch that breaks, sending him sprawling. He spends much of the rest of our laborious walk downstream as we clamber over and under rusty barbed wire fences ruminating aloud on the recent fatal heart attack of an acquaintance of his, a barber. Lack of exercise, I suggest. Ricardo came back to live here after years of working in Denver, where he claims the pollution finally drove him away. "I couldn't breathe there because of the pollution," he once told me, pronouncing the last word with relishing deliberation. He is a stocky man in his early or middle forties and seems content to pass his life trout fishing between odd jobs like this.

The channel begins to drop, and between low grassy banks at the bottom end of pastureland the water flows more rapidly now. To the river side, large junipers line the ditch. It is alpine through here, lush, bright, splashing. Branches and twigs are easier to fish out. The ground is more open and less treacherous. The last property before the lower *desagüe* is a well-mowed grassy plot presided over by a large, unfinished two-story adobe the owner has been working on for three or four years now. The round structure is still unlived in, and rarely is anyone here when I come through. The owner has given me permission to use his long driveway down from Los Cerritos whenever I want to check the *desagüe* by car, which saves a lot of tramping through wet pastureland along the ditch. No one is here today. We follow the ditch through the lawn and past a barbecue grill and a metal lawn table and chairs and round a bend to the lower *desagüe,* which has become clogged with the branches and weeds we have dislodged during our morning's labor. After cleaning the trash out of the cement works, I drop a two-by-six pine plank into the *desagüe* channel and raise the gate into the ditch, letting the water pass. There are two schools of thought about how much water you put into the ditch the first days of the season: either a lot, so that the leaves and twigs blowing into the channel during the winds of late March will be swept along so rapidly that they will not jam up and cause the banks to overflow or even collapse—or only a little water, so that when the ditch blocks up, as inevitably it will somewhere along the line, there won't be so much water in the channel that it will flood over the banks—which all amounts to six of one, half a dozen of the other. I decide to put in a medium amount of water. As the ground is still wet nobody will be irrigating for a few weeks, and the winds have not been severe in the two days since we dug out the ditch: the channel should still be fairly clear.

From now on our main work in bringing the water down will be to station ourselves at the various culverts along the way and to fork out the debris as it is pushed along by the water. We set out across the pasture toward Leandro Castillo's house. The first place we stop is at the sharp bend at his pigpen. The water reaches that point just as we do. We fork and rake out a foaming pad of brown leaves and grey cottonwood twigs that are jamming up at the bend and then walk on down the grassy bank past Leandro's well-kept lawn where his German shepherd has taken a stand to bark at us, and move on rapidly toward the highway to position ourselves at the culvert under the road before the water reaches it. Stationing ourselves on the banks opposite each other, we let the water flow into our tools and then fork out the debris—or as much as we can, since there is always too much to catch—and run across the highway to the mouth of the siphon. Early this morning I came up here and drove a half-dozen three-foot sections of re-bar into the ground just in front of the siphon to form a crude grate, which proves now to be quite effective in catching debris and gives us more time to fork it out.

With that I can dispense with Ricardo's help, or at least I think I can. I write out a *papelito* for his hours and suggest he wait a week or so before taking it to the treasurer, by which time the commission will have collected *delincuencias* from this and past years' cleanings and *mayordomia* for the new season. There are four or five places where I'll station myself at the ditch to await the water: I can reach them all by driving most of the way. The first is a culvert under the gravel driveway of the Thompson place whose fields I rent, three places down from the siphon. I reach it just as the water is arriving and jump out of the truck and fork out a small pile of debris, catching perhaps half of it. The rest sails on down the ditch.

Next, my place, a quarter of a mile down the lane. I park the truck at the house and climb up the fifteen-foot bank to the ditch and follow it upriver to the next property, the Gregory Serna place, where the break in the bank was. Pitchfork in hand, I walk up the winding channel to meet the descending water. By the time it gets here the flow will be pushing a large roll of debris, and I will walk it back down through my place and into the next if need be, to fork out as much as I can. The ditch is about four feet wide through here. The fine sand on the bottom glares in the sun. All is quiet. This is a strange wait, as if for a train on tracks that curve out of sight behind a hill or for a bus on a mountain highway: something will arrive here at this place by the means of this channel, soon, perhaps very soon, unless something has gone wrong up there–a tree could have fallen across the ditch, a bank could have collapsed. I am about to walk a little further up when a brown and grey tongue slips into view around a bend and rolls toward me, its dry leaves hissing softly, twigs snapping, approaching like some creature, a giant snake that has assumed a somewhat disorderly disguise. It travels along at perhaps two miles an hour. You can keep ahead of it unless you are trying to fork out the debris, and then it is traveling much too fast. I retreat to where the ditch bank is low and clear, climb up and begin forking my way down with the water, trying to get the largest branches out first. Here and there the tongue pauses, jammed by a dam of its own making until freed of its own accord or until my efforts release it. The water behind the first twenty feet of floating dry leaves is the brown of coffee and cream. Through the hundred and fifty feet of my place I manage to fish out most of the larger branches and many of the matted weeds. I let it go at the fenceline: I'll catch it at the next culvert another quarter of a mile down the road. The water flows past where I stand: a train, a ribbon, a rope, a belt that will run and flow for another seven months. The surrounding landscape is still largely dormant, only the grasses in protected spots are sending out points into the warming air. With this water spring-time can begin in the fields and orchards below. Suddenly it is here.

The next construction is a short drive down to Wilfred Ortiz's place, up behind his collection of dere-lict cars and trucks, and across a *canoa* or flume by which the ditch traverses a small arroyo. The channel narrows sharply as it enters the *canoa,* a gutterlike structure of sheetmetal supported by juniper posts set in the sand, less than two feet wide. It is well sloped, however, so that once water enters, it flows rapidly across the span. The mouth is one of the places that has to be checked when I bring the water down and then periodically throughout the summer. When I arrive the water is not yet there and I set out again to meet it, remembering too late that there is a culvert I forgot about on the next property up. Then I realize that the bank is very high along there; even if the culvert did plug up, the water would still stay in the channel. Two of the largest places on the ditch lie along here, Wilfred Ortiz's, six to eight acres, and immediately up river from it, his uncle Francisco "Paco" Ortiz's. They are not on speaking terms at the moment, I think. Wilfred is generally considered a water hog. In the many times I have checked his two ditch gates I have never found them closed. Wilfred uses the ditch as a perpetual spring, letting the water run down over his eroded sandy pastures back into the river. In the now distant past he and I held a half-hour shouting match over the phone about some minor ditch matter, and he and his wife Leonore later bested me in an argument regarding an undated receipt I carelessly issued them once as secretary–treasurer, forcing the ditch (as I saw it) to credit work done one year against *delincuencias* run up in a later year. But we are now on friendlier terms, perhaps because I make a point of hiring some of his relatives up the ditch for our various harvest jobs on the farm. And to his credit, he always sends workers to the spring cleaning. His place is two *piones,* which means he must supply two workers for every job as well as pay twice the *mayordomia* of most members. Whenever he complains of the fees I always suggest that he ask the commission to reduce his place to one *pión,* but he never has, perhaps in the fear that he might then have to change his prodigal irrigating habits.

On the Acequia de la Jara even the dead still serve. The property a few yards upriver from where I am standing, that of Paco Ortiz, is listed under the name of his long dead father, Lauriano. There are six or seven surviving Ortiz sons and daughters, all in their fifties and sixties now, and though the property belongs to them all, Paco is the only one living in the old grey cement-plastered adobe, in the company of a large color TV. A Social Security or Korean War military disability pension gives him enough to live on without having to work. Adjoining Wilfred's on the east, Paco's is the largest place on our ditch. For several years its main field was planted in wheat and corn by a neighbor, but it now stands empty of all but patches of volunteer wheat, wild sunflower, Russian thistle.

Paco served as *mayordomo* during two of the driest seasons I have known here. As *mayordomo* he was the opposite of Reynaldo, good at keeping the ditch running during the summer even under difficult conditions, but terrible at supervising the spring cleaning. He would mark off the *tareas* well enough, but then he would retreat to the end of the line and joke away in Spanish and English with the end *piones* in a nonstop patter of the Paul Harvey vein. When a commissioner once suggested to Paco that he might think of actually inspecting the line, he replied in his rasping smoker's voice, "You must think I'm crazy—you want me to go in there and get beat up?" followed by coughing guffaws. Yet during the irrigation season he regulated the water with great care and was very conscientious about checking the *desagües* and the *presa* at least once a week. As *mayordomo,* he was a mixture of the strong-willed and the timid. If you wanted him to do something, you had to prepare yourself to hear all the arguments for why your idea was unwise, untimely, untraditional and pointless anyway—with asides on how Johnson, Nixon, Ford, Carter, or Reagan had once taken him or would eventually drive him to the poorhouse. But if you stuck to your guns he would finally give in. "Well, if that's what you want to do, then I guess we'd better get to work on it."

Through the three *mayordomos* I worked with as a commissioner, technically speaking all of them employees of the *comisión,* I gradually discovered an important fact of local life: though the *mayordomo* is in charge of the ditch, no one is really in charge of him. *Mayordomos* have a reputation of being independent, stubborn, difficult, which Juliana Espinosa, one of the first women *mayordomas,* has held to in recent years on the other side of the valley. And though the commission is supposed to oversee the *mayordomo,* in my experience this has more often meant trying to coax work out of him with the carrot of a paltry sal-

ary while at the same time extracting money from the
parciantes in order to pay the *mayordomo,* and the commission playing the thankless role of intermediary
who often gets it from both sides, especially in a dry
year—while the *mayordomo,* if he is clever enough to
realize that usually no one else wants the job, only
need deal with the river once the cleaning is over,
with beavers and muskrats, and the occasional trouble-
some *parciante,* and usually in his own good time.
Man, Nietzsche observed, has no reason to be angry
at nature: anger comes only from dealings with other
men. After ten years of *andando colectando,* collecting
ditch fees from my neighbors, smoothing over ruffled
feelings and promising water to *parciantes* I then had
to beg the *mayordomo* to deliver, to have become *mayordomo* myself proved to be an unexpected relief.
Suddenly everything was much simpler. Whenever I
wanted more water in the ditch I just went and got it,
without asking or conferring with anyone, and whenever I thought it was running too high I could go and
turn it down without asking someone else to do it.
Even the pay wasn't bad. My first year I kept a log
of my time, which averaged ten hours a month over
the season, or about ten dollars an hour, better than I
make per hour at most other things I do.

The hissing tongue appears around a bend. The
culvert upstream must be okay. I station myself at the
mouth of the *canoa* and fork out what seems like an

endless jam of leaves, twigs, branches, tumbleweeds. The water passes. I can follow it easily enough through Wilfred's backyard past the wide-eyed stare of abandoned cars from the late 1950s—the ground is clear through here—and then down to the next property, forking as I go, catching the largest pieces of debris. From then on the ditch runs steeply downhill along a narrow channel set high on the side of the hill back of a half-dozen houses, toward the last culvert by which it passes under Reynaldo Vasques's driveway. To get there, I have to drive back upriver to the highway and then down through the village to the school, then down a dirt road to a bridge back across the river, a five-minute drive. By the time I get to the one-lane bridge I decide to check the water at Ewaldo Serrano's place just opposite, and I drive up past his brother's house—Orlando Serrano is part of this four-house complex of the Serrano clan—and park behind Ewaldo's garage on a plot of recently burned-over ground. Ewaldo, who must be in his seventies, is a big broad man who speaks no English. He is very faithful to the ditch, turns out for all occasions. We are both a little afraid of each other. He is perhaps embarrassed that he speaks no English, and I embarrassed that my Spanish is not very good. He speaks Spanish in a deep voice both nasal and guttural, perhaps a very pure and unschooled form of the local variant; there is also something Indian in his broad dark face with prominent cheekbones and hooded eyes and even perhaps in the nasalness of his speech. He is a kindly, gentle man without a trace of the steaming *machismo* of some Hispanic males—or the haughtiness that old age can turn it into. Sympathetically, however, we communicate on another level, as must those who share at heart a common purpose. Several weeks ago when I drove around to tell *parciantes* who I wanted to come and cut willows, *cortar la jara,* the week before we were to dig out the ditch—work which needs only ten or twelve *piones,* not all thirty—Ewaldo was standing up here by his garage, while I had stopped my truck a hundred yards below to ask Orlando to show up for willow cutting if he wanted to further reduce his old *delincuencias*. Traditionally the cutting of the *jara* is work given to the old men, and Ewaldo always showed up for it. Seeing him standing up on the knoll above us, where he was perhaps wondering what business I was on for the ditch, I got out of the truck and waved up to him and then raised my arms with my fists tight and opened and closed them as if manipulating long-handled pruning shears and called out: "¡*Mañana!*" He nodded his head in understanding and walked out of sight into his garage.

This afternoon no one is around at any of the four Serrano houses, two of them adobes, two of them mobile homes. I walk up through the burned-over land behind Ewaldo's garage and house and climb up on the ditch bank and wait. The channel is steep and wide along here where it crosses the course of a small arroyo that very occasionally runs enough to silt up the ditch for a short distance. The water is prompt in arriving and I follow it around the serpentine bends of this open stretch, forking as I go.

One more stop at Reynaldo's driveway and that will be it. His culvert is somewhat squashed from the incessant traffic of his family of thirteen grown children and their husbands and wives, plus the occasional propane tanker, but the slope is good and the water passes rapidly through the tunnel once I have fished out the worst of the debris. From here on the ditch tumbles down a steep gully to the willow-grown pastureland of the last *parciante,* the channel ending abruptly in a grove of cottonwoods. From there the water fans out through the grass and trees. I have never walked across to see where it must trickle finally back into the river. It is four in the afternoon by the time I get home, bone-weary from the walking, the work with the pitchfork and rake, the bending over, the getting in and out of the truck. Animals need to be fed, a fire laid, other chores. I know I should climb up the bank and follow the ditch up into the Gregory Serna place to see how the repaired break is doing, but I don't. I'm sure it's all right. We did a good job, didn't we? Or did we? I am too tired to climb up that bank one more time. It is almost dark when I step out the door after dinner to get something out of the truck. I know the sound. I have heard it a dozen times. It is unmistakable, a higher, more showering pitch than the low washing roar of the river, and closer, too: it is the sound of a waterfall. The ditch has broken. I run back into the house, shout out the news to the family, pull on my boots, grab a flashlight, try to remember where I left the shovel. Still in the truck? After all these years, why do I still forget where I have left the shovel at the end of the day? The time must be about eight in the evening. The ditch has been running for all of four hours.

My headlights pick out the water just beginning to wash across the driveway into my field from next door, meaning—I hope—that the break is still young. A vision haunts me: that whole section, thirty feet of it, fallen away in a slab into the field below, the labor of thirty men working for an hour or more crashing down into the brush. At worst this will mean summoning a large crew to spend a day digging a whole new channel through four feet of clay and roots further back into the hillside. At the highway I turn left uphill toward Los Cerritos. Times like this I am grateful for Nick Manzanares's permission to use his long driveway to get to the lower *desagüe,* though I wish we had the new one now next to the highway. This is the way the ditch is. You work yourself half to death and think everything's fine. But it isn't. It never is. The ditch is a moody creature, unpredictable, irritable, irritating, unreliable, particularly this time of year when the river's rising and the wind blows dead branches off the cottonwoods all the time. I know I should have made that last effort to climb the ditch bank and check on the old break. What would I have seen? A leak? Then what would I have done? Worried. Perhaps decided to shut the water off before dark. Let the newly dug earth settle. Tramp it down. Perhaps I would have seen nothing, thought it was just fine. Should I feel guilty? No, just tired. Just tired is enough to feel right now.

Nick's house is dark. Shovel and dim flashlight in hand, I cross his lawn. I know the path almost by feel, having traversed it so many times night and day, in clear weather and storm, through all the seasons: across the plank over the ditch, through the opening in the low fence, along the stone ledge parallel to the ditch, through the narrow gap between a cottonwood and a fence post, through some low saplings, the leap across the rocks to the crumbling cement structure. At the *desagüe* I slip the shovel blade under the splashboard and pry it up, sending the water all back into the river again, then drop the gate closed across the mouth of the ditch channel. But this, I know, is not enough. I wasn't thorough a couple of hours ago, so this time I ought to be. I feel my way along the bank and shovel back in the pile of sand, replacing the berm across the channel. Lastly, I drop into place a crude, ill-fitting wooden gate at the mouth of the *desagüe* which forces more of the water to run over the stone bank back to the river.

It is dark. Before I was tired but content. Now I am

worn out and discouraged. This is Monday evening. The ditch will take four or five days to dry out enough that we can work on it again. Perhaps next weekend. In bad years in the past we usually got at least a couple of days of water before the ditch broke the first time, not just four hours.

Some ditch. Some *mayordomo*.

Breaks. Recollections of countless other breaks drift through my mind as I lie in bed later that night, too tense with exhaustion to sleep. There was the time ten or eleven years ago when my wife and I decided to take our first day off in months from the farm and from building our adobe house. We drove away and found a river to sit beside in another valley far from the landscape our labor had engraved in our minds. Returning at the end of the summer day, we stopped at the Thompsons' to pick up the kids. "Something terrible has happened," Penelope Thompson blurted out, rushing up to us as we climbed out of the car. "The ditch broke. But everything's all right." Despite the last protestation, we imagined the house filled with mud and water. The walls of an adobe house, if sufficiently dampened, melt into mud pies. We rushed home. The house was dry. But the whole of our two acres below it had been thoroughly irrigated, a little heavily here and there, but even rows of lettuce seedlings had survived the flood. The break had been right behind our new tool shed built of ponderosa poles, where a ten-foot-long section of bank undermined by muskrats or crayfish had slid away. Another time, a few years ago in early October, I awoke just before dawn and looked out our bedroom window and wondered why the starry sky was reflected on the ground. Then I heard the sound of rushing water, that faint waterfall. Our small tool shed was now a large pole barn where we stored our equipment, supplies, produce. I pulled on my boots and rushed into the dark. There was water all over the driveway and all through the shed. I called to my wife and jumped into the truck and raced up to the stop sign at the highway. From there I had to walk in. Nick Manzanares had not yet begun building his house and there was no road down to the *desagüe* from Los Cerritos. Leandro Castillo's large and ferocious German shepherd fortunately slept soundly that night. I have very poor night vision. The flashlight batteries were nearly dead and I saw myself as a character in one of those old Eveready advertisements featuring illustrated accounts of fire, flood, downed power lines in which that brand's batteries or flashlights had made the difference between life and death. As they might now, because the batteries were about to burn out. There would be cows—a bull, perhaps—in the next field. With the help of the brownish beam I managed to reach the *desagüe* and turn the water back into the river and struggle back through the sodden pasture and three barbed-wire fences in the dark without so much as scratching myself. Back home, I waded through the shed helping my wife rescue the last of the tools, seed, fertilizer from the flood during the next half hour it took for the last of the water to drain from the ditch. At about five the water trickled into silence. The break was just across the fence on Gregory Serna's place, just up from the last one. The shed looked terrible with all its contents piled up on boxes and lumber and benches, but later it turned out that there had been very little damage. The morning was cold and our wet hands and feet were freezing. There was nothing else we needed to do out in the shed, we could go back inside the house and warm ourselves with some tea and climb back into bed under our one luxury at the time, an electric blanket. As we stepped out of the shed two things—surely unconnected— happened at once: a meteorite arced down across the faintly blue western sky, and all the lights went out. And stayed out until sunrise as we lay in bed shivering, blankets and coats heaped on top of us.

Finally I relax. Sleep seems possible. A thought promises to release me: tonight at least I don't have to worry anymore about the ditch. It has already broken.

Four

Along the section of the ditch which runs from back of our shed upriver though most of Gregory Serna's place, a stretch where it clings tenuously to the side of the hill and where the downside bank is neither very high nor thick, perfect for muskrats to construct their own subterranean water systems, their little *desagües,* the bank has collapsed seven or eight times over the past ten years, often spring and fall of the same year. The ditch perches along the hillside ten to fifteen feet straight above the bottomland where we have built our house and shed and where Gregory Serna's father planted the now neglected Red Delicious apple trees next door. I doubt the creatures responsible for the breaks have benefited by them—in fact, they must often be drowned or suffocated or crushed under the tons of earth and water that slide down into the fields below. I have never seen the actual creature along here, but its works on the section we repaired while cleaning the ditch Friday, just up from the breaks that flooded the shed years ago, were the most extensive I have ever seen. They began in the center of the ditch bed with a narrow fissure that ran for thirty or forty feet down the center of the channel, widening as it went, toward what was probably the main burrow, a series of chambers strung with reddish and brownish roots underlying the whole bed, and which the creature maintained and extended, I imagine, by directing the subterranean trickle—increasingly a flow—here and there toward an outlet low on the outside of the ditch bank, to a drain, a *desagüe*. In the summer, when you walk the ditch bank—where you can walk it—on a quiet morning you can hear the water leaking from these places. But as the muskrats—there would be a pair, they would bear young—expanded their burrow they would also increase their risks. A first labor might be in establishing a small flow through a tunnel starting in the bottom or at the side of the ditch beneath the water line and ending lower down on the outside of the bank, while as the works became larger the problem might reverse itself—how to control and even reduce a flow that erosion would be making greater every day, particularly when the ditch is running high and fast. But these are water creatures—and the more water the merrier. Until suddenly the flow becomes a torrent and roofs fall in and walls collapse and everything plunges down into the orchard below, twenty feet of ditch bank crumbling away and carrying rocks and brush with it, everything then pounded and dissolved by a loud pursuing waterfall.

The Gregory Serna place, where most of these breaks occur, consists of six acres of apples overgrown with willow and wild rose and bordered along the dirt road by the river by an attractive stand of narrow-leaf cottonwoods. Serna comes down from his job in Colorado once or twice a year to supervise the pruning of the apple trees—they rarely bear fruit, being otherwise neglected—and to lament over the encroaching thickets of brush. Every several years he runs a tractor-pulled disk over the willows, no doubt stimulating them to send out new runners. His place has become a kind of wildlife refuge. The skunks our dogs often encounter live there, and last winter at night I often heard the high-pitched chattering of foxes or coyotes across the fence. When we had goats I used to cut willows for them across there and once, in sandals, I narrowly missed stepping on a small sidewinder in the grass—but so intently was it moving that it didn't notice my presence inches away. Several years ago the willows along the ditch had grown into a thick intertwining canopy that made digging nearly impossible. With Serna's permission the commission arranged for the local volunteer fire department to make a controlled burn along his section of the ditch, as a practice drill for the firemen. Since then, digging out and even widening the ditch slightly has proven much easier.

The Serna place is where I imagine the creature in Kafka's "The Burrow" must live, tunneling away in search of ultimate security. Our collapsed ditch banks may be how that unfinished tale ends—in a gaping hole strung by root filaments and stood over by a man with a shovel in the bright morning light. The break—the new break, last night's—is far less serious than I had feared. The original collapse last fall occurred at a bend where the ditch elbows out toward the field, and in repairing it Friday we cut a new channel across the bend, straightening it. But apparently we failed to pack down the earth sufficiently where the old channel with its fissures in the bed passes through the new bank, and we must have left an air pocket or a crack which the water fingered its way into and widened out to what is now a hole about two feet in diameter. I would have been writing *papelitos* at the end of the workday Friday: I must have forgotten to inspect this crucial section of the new bank. But the damage is not so bad. At most, I will need four or five men to make the repair. The channel must be moved back into the hillside a foot or two along seven or eight feet of the bank or whatever will give us enough dirt to fill up the hole and move the channel into firmer ground.

I call up a crew for next Saturday but the week turns out to be cold and wet, so it is early the following week before we can do the work. Reynaldo Vasques still owes a little on his place, and I ask his brother next door also, who sends Billy Serrano to work for him, and the last *parciante* on the ditch, who sends his thirty-five-year-old son, Porfirio Serna, who now lives on the place and who I have never worked with before. As we gather up at the break at the appointed hour I feel the eyes of someone saying I am a newcomer upstart here, though in fact I have spent as much of my adult life—perhaps more— in the valley as Porfirio Serna has. In the intervening ten days no signs of new excavations have been cast up in the area of the break. I suspect the muskrats did not survive the October collapse, or else they moved up the ditch and began digging a new burrow. Though I am ostensibly in charge, Reynaldo Vasques's suggestions and directions take precedence. He has dealt with these problems thirty or forty years longer than I have. He and Porfirio, neighbors now, are talking away busily in Spanish. I find this of interest as Reynaldo and Porfirio's father, a man in his seventies now, have never been on good terms, at least in my hearing, the lower neighbor commonly accusing the upper of never letting any water pass downstream to his place and then of dumping trash into it whenever he rarely does. Perhaps some reconciliation is taking place. Certain conversations have a ritualistic cast. This one, between the thirty-five-year-old and the sixty-five-year-old, seems to be running toward the way things once were, the way they used to be. The words *niños,* children, and *respeto,* respect, pass back and forth. We all pause in our digging. The younger generation has become the subject of complaint. I interject a word in English. "You know," Porfirio turns to me, "the problem today is the young people have no respect." Silently, I wonder what they should respect. Porfirio speaks English in a slow ponderous manner, as if delivering unquestionable truths. He is a beefy fellow with a big pot belly and protruding lips. "Now you take someone like Reynaldo. He raised his children the right way, so they would respect him. This man knew how to control his children with his eyes, by the way he looked at them." I glance at Reynaldo. He gives a sly little smile, not unproud. "He could get his kids to do whatever he wanted just by the way he looked at them."

Respect, authority, firmness, the flag, uniforms. So goes the drift of the conversation as we resume digging. And then everything began to fall apart during the war in Vietnam, according to Porfirio. I suggest without insisting that it was hard to respect a government—if governments should ever be respected—that was lying about a messy pointless war. But I am ill at ease arguing along these lines; I wish I had let the ritualistic exchange continue without my comments.

"Today," Porfirio carries on, undeterred by my objections, "the kids get everything they want, cars, tele-
vision, stereos, they don't have to listen to us. In the
old days everybody had to work. Everybody had to.
There wasn't anything." Reynaldo agrees, nodding,
then adds in his reedy, quavering voice: "We used to
go to town to shop twice a year, once in the winter
and once in the summer. We used to take our wagon
to town and buy a thousand pounds of flour to last
half a year." Town is twenty-five miles away. In the old
days there was a narrow-gauge railway line with a
daily train in each direction that stopped a couple of
miles down the Rio Grande, but that would have cost
money. I sometimes think that nowadays most people
in the village drive to town and back at least once a
day, seven days a week, sometimes twice a day. "And
when we went to pick peas in Colorado it took us five
days to get there in our wagons, to Monte Vista." Today by car: six hours, say, perhaps less.

"What about school?" I ask Reynaldo. "Did you go
to school?"

"One month a year. December, sometimes February."

"How far did you get?"

"Fourth grade," he smiles. "All the nuns taught us
was how to pray." This would have been around the
time of the depression.

I ask him about the age of the ditch, which will
someday be of importance in establishing what are

called priority dates for all nine ditches in the valley, when our water is adjudicated in the courts. Adjudication is the legal process by which the state government sues individual property owners to establish their surface water rights, and this portion of the Rio de la Junta has not yet been submitted to the prolonged and divisive legal battles adjudication almost always entails. In adjudicated streams, when the water gets low, the ditch with the oldest priority date—that is, the oldest ditch as established by whatever documentation still exists—gets to take as much water as it has a right to, leaving whatever is left over for the ditch with the next oldest priority date, and so on down the line. I hope that when the time comes all the ditches can be persuaded to pool their priority dates so that the traditional water-sharing agreement will hold over into the new era of adjudicated water, whenever it begins. Adjudication suits are becoming more and more costly for the state to pursue and are taking longer to resolve, in part because landowners are far better organized than they used to be; it may be years or even decades before the elaborate legal process is begun by which our segment of the river is turned into a marketable commodity that can be transferred from place to place regardless of the way its waters until then have traditionally flowed. At present, at least in theory, surface water in the valley can be bought and sold—as in theory land or cars without legal titles can be. Adjudication will give each property owner on every ditch a piece of paper, a deed, if you will, a water right that can then be sold or rented out or leased to anyone else, anywhere else within the state—subject to the approval of the Office of the State Engineer. But until adjudication, water will stay here with us in the valley, on paper and in the river, under the patchwork of state, federal, and traditional Spanish water laws under which we operate the ditches.

In times of low water the traditional water agreement among the ditches of the valley divided the ditches into two groups, the upper and the lower, and presumed that when the river started going down, usually in late June and again often in August and even again in October, then the upper four ditches would tend to take more water than they let pass to the lower three, so that when the time came to divide the river the lower ditches, the first to suffer, would take the water first and keep it a day longer each week than the upper ditches, that is, four days out of seven. The details of this arrangement were never committed to writing, and partly as a result many hours, even days, were spent by the commissions of the seven ditches in arguing about how bad the drought was or which ditch was suffering the most, how much water the upper ditches were going to let pass to the lower ones—with convoys of cars and trucks driving from house to house in the heat of the afternoon or early evening, and everyone becoming more exasperated and impatient with each passing day without rain. The ritual argument of the upper ditches was always: "You must give us more notice—a week's notice—before you come to take the water." And the lower ditches, and our ditch, the Acequia de la Jara, is the lowermost of the lower (excepting an eighth ditch, the Acequia del Pueblo, which is fed by springs above the highway but which off and on participated in the negotiations as a lower ditch), always responded: "But the upper ditches take all the water anyway without consulting us, without giving us any advance notice." The upper ditches also used to argue to be left a small amount of water "for the chickens"— or for those *parciantes* who until the advent of a community drinking water system a few years ago still used water from one ditch in particular for household purposes. The lower ditches countered with the claim that when the upper ditches' turn for the river came they never let a drop go by to the lower ditches during those three days, that the lower ditches never had the luxury of water "for the chickens."

Several springs ago I took the initiative in organizing a gathering of all the commissions to draft a written agreement to resolve in part the two areas of long-standing dispute, advance notice and water for the chickens. After an evening in the local school of rehashing all the old arguments we agreed on a text which stipulated that the water sharing could be triggered at any time by the commission of any lower

ditch requesting the commission of any upper ditch
to put it into effect, as long as the request was made
a week in advance of whatever Sunday morning at
eight the lower ditches wished to shut off the upper
ditches and move the water down to their headgates;
and in exchange for advance notice the upper ditches
agreed, if reluctantly, not to press their claim for
water for the chickens. And in general everybody at
the meeting seemed to see that the lower ditches were
far better off to ask for the water before everyone was
desperate, so that all the ditches would have enough
time to readjust their schedules and accustom their
mayordomos and *parciantes* to the prospect of scarcity.

Adjudication of our water, whenever the State Engineer decides to set the machinery in motion, could
threaten our river-sharing agreement by which, despite countless disputes, the seven ditches have managed to cooperate with each other during dry months
for as many years as I have lived here and surely many
more before my time. The agreement is founded on
an assumed equality among all the ditches—though
the upper ditches, always rich in water, are vaguely
considered morally superior to the lower ditches,
often poor in water—an equality which may well be
undermined when the adjudication process estab-
lishes a hierarchy based on priority dates, on dates
established by documentation, largely the result of
what few pieces of paper have chanced to survive over
the centuries. I am interested in the antiquity of our

ditch for a very practical reason: where it would place us in the hierarchy of future priority dates. Reynaldo maintains that ours has been here since the time of his grandparents or before and now tells me, as we are digging away, that he has a "paper" in his house which says that our ditch is the oldest in the valley. But I am skeptical—this is the most sparsely settled side of the valley, and perhaps a third of the *parciantes* now living over here have moved in since my wife and I arrived sixteen years ago. If anything, I would guess the Acequia de la Jara is among the younger of the ditches. But someday, I tell Reynaldo, I would like to have a look at that paper of his.

Reynaldo asks me whether I have ever heard of the *palas de tabla*. Yes, I have, years ago. In the very old days (in the version I was told) ditch-cleaning crews were divided up into two groups for the spring cleaning. One group was sent up into the mountains to cut down oak trees and carve *palas de tabla,* wooden shovels, for the crew down below actually digging out the ditch. The *palas de tabla* presumably wore out very fast or frequently broke, hence the need to have them being made continuously up in the mountains while the ditch was being dug out. But I explain to Reynaldo why over the years of reflecting on the charming story I had come to the conclusion that it did not entirely make sense. To begin with I had never seen an oak tree in New Mexico that you could make anything recognizable as a shovel from—the local scrub oak that grows around seven thousand feet and above is simply too small. But of course you might be able to make a reasonable shovel out of green pine, even aspen. And though iron might then have been a valued substance it nevertheless would have been common in horseshoes, nails, axes, saws (to cut the trees), and—why not?—iron shovel blades. And a blacksmith would have been a common feature of any agricultural settlement, and indeed probably every village had its own blacksmith up until perhaps the 1940s. "Where *la fraga* used to be" is still a landmark in the valley for everybody over a certain age.

Through all of this Billy Serrano has been uncharacteristically quiet, perhaps from a hangover. He is a small unhealthy-looking man well into his forties, with cloudy blue eyes slightly wall-eyed, a scraggly black beard on a long oval face of prematurely weathered skin, a bent and perhaps broken nose through which he apparently cannot breathe, which gives his voice a flat, almost choking quality. He speaks English with a vaguely western accent, suggesting that he left home at an early age and grew up among Anglos. He is dressed today in tattered sneakers and a dirty brown quilted jacket. He and his wife came back from Colorado or Utah about five years ago and live in a small rented house in Los Cerritos. He drives an old Chevy pickup painted primer brown, which does not run for long periods of time, and he and his wife often have to walk the two miles to and from the village store. There are many poor people in our village, but they are among the few landless poor. In the past he has been annoyingly obsequious around me, with the object of playing out work crews so that he would make a few dollars more that day, but this year he has been less insistent. And I am beginning to appreciate the fact that he does actually show up for work and is not a shirker. When he first turned up at the spring cleaning five years ago he brought his son Billy Junior, a quick and hard-working kid with bleeding gums, and I hired both of them to work for the ditch rather than for individual *parciantes*. At the end of the day, while writing out the checks, I asked Billy Senior whether they wanted one check or two—and the father said yes, one check would be fine, but was interrupted by the son who said firmly that he wanted his own check, thank you. In that moment I glimpsed what might be the character of their home life. Since then I have made a point of asking Billy Senior about his son, who moved—or ran—away at an early age and now works in Colorado. Today it occurs to me that I don't know who they are related to here in the valley, if anyone—I don't even know if he is originally from here. Serrano is one of the two most common surnames in the area. I ask him.

"Did you know Tancredo Serrano?" he asks back. I nod. "He was my father."

"Who lived across the river?"

"Yeah."

Of course. Now I see. Tancredo was a little man too with a wizened look and a diverted septum and a way of talking through lips held almost rigid, talking with his tongue more than his lips. He died perhaps seven years ago, 1978 or 1979. Also a walker, Tancredo, because he didn't have a car, didn't know how to drive. I often drove him back from the store with his two bags of groceries. He too was a brown leathery man with black hair. In his old age he had a sweet disposition, was pleased to speak with me in Spanish, and once very ceremoniously brought me into his house (where I met his wife the only time) to show me a wonder of early technology, a wood cookstove with a water jacket and hot water tank hooked up to it about which I questioned him in detail. Tancredo was the last man in the village to work a team of horses and a wagon, and when my wife and I were building the first rooms of our house he drove it down into La Jara to pick up some kindling along the river and then right up our driveway to where we were laying adobes. Standing up in the wagon and holding the reins of the two horses, he doffed his grey hat and politely asked us whether we might be interested in buying the team and wagon. No, unfortunately, we weren't. I knew nothing of horses and had always been shy of them, and what could we do with the wagon but turn it into a decorative yard piece, a sad fate for something still obviously functional. Perhaps we all knew that there was nobody left now to buy his team and wagon, now that he was getting too old to use them as he always had, to drive up the arroyos to the mesa tops for firewood, as his ancestors had done for generations. He did not insist. He probably thought he should try those unpredictable young newcomers who were moving into the valley and doing strange things like building houses out of the mud bricks that were then, for a short time at least, very much out of fashion among his own people. We watched him turn the wagon around, a four-wheeled vehicle with wooden spoke wheels and a bed with low sides, and make his way slowly down our rutted driveway to the turn onto the dirt road that ran along the river back up toward the highway. Through the cottonwoods bordering the Serna place we watched Tancredo sitting erect in his faded blue work shirt on the seat of the wagon disappear up the road behind the two plodding horses. It may have been the last time he took the team out. I no longer remember the sound of the wagon creaking or of iron wheels rolling across the dirt. But I remember thinking that this was something I would probably never see again or hear in my life in quite this way. The past of this place had come, in the form of old Tancredo Serrano, to make a request of me—this was how I later came to think of that moment.

I told this story to Billy as we worked. He listened without emotion, said nothing. I couldn't remember seeing his truck at his mother's place in recent years, if I ever had. Perhaps they were estranged. The old ones live to an old age because they are tough, I imagine, however sweet and good-natured they can become in their last years; perhaps Tancredo had driven away his son by the ferociousness of his look as a younger father, as backed up by old-fashioned beatings of the sort Porfirio might approve of. Billy said nothing. He said he knew nothing of the broken hip that preceded his father's death.

Reynaldo is talking to Porfirio. "People don't believe me," he's saying, "when I tell them I still use a horse for plowing." He must be the last one in the valley. There are a few old farmers still using horses up in the higher valleys where the internal combustion engine arrived a decade later than here. The horse has its advantages. Like you it tires with work, needs rest, food, water: your rhythms are similar. A tractor, a machine, invites you to work at a pace unnatural to the body, and while the machine does the work faster and better in some ways it is also designed with complex needs that seem like deep ulterior purposes to connect you to international fossil fuel and manufacturing conglomerates, banks, insurance companies; and its waste products, unlike a horse's, are toxic and useless. Reynaldo's horse is connected to his fields through what it eats and excretes, in addition to the labor it produces, and through his own history and traditions it is connected to other individuals who own and breed horses as draft animals; and what

Reynaldo might spend in veterinary fees and hay and grain is probably far less than what I put out each year for fuel, oil, filters, replacement parts, interest, insurance. The difference between the modern world, which Tancredo Serrano did not really have to enter, and the world which it has almost completely displaced throughout much of this region, and relatively recently, lies largely in the nature of such connections—whether they are close and local and among near equals, or remote and seemingly abstract and between individuals and vastly larger institutions. The four of us here today, piling the last shovelfuls of reddish earth on top of the rebuilt bank late in the morning of a spring day, a weekday, at an hour when most of our neighbors are at work in town, in their classrooms, in their clinics and hospitals, at the laboratory facilities in Los Alamos, in the welfare and unemployment and food-stamp offices, where they work day after day, five days a week, and where they will work for the twenty-five or thirty-five years it will take to earn their retirement—in contrast, the four of us on the other side of things, on the side of the traditional way, a generation or more—whatever our ages—behind the times in which we live. For Billy, Reynaldo, and Porfirio this may be less a matter of choice than of fate—they have all had forays into the other world as servicemen, miners, construction workers—while for myself it was a matter of choice at one time but which over the years has come to seem not unlike their fate: things have not worked out for me in that other world, the contemporary institutional one. And here I am. Here we are. Digging out a ditch, that now not unpleasant labor which as a child was held up to me as representing the very bottom of the social heap, in such phrases as: "Unless you want to spend your life digging ditches. . . ."

Before we part, Reynaldo asks whether I will need any help in bringing the water down again. I thank him, but no, I can do it myself. It will be easier this time. There has been some wind this week with the storm, but I'm sure the worst of the trash was swept out of the ditch during the four-hour run last Monday. After pausing for a cup of coffee at the house I drive up to the lower *desagüe* and turn the water back into the ditch and check the culverts between there and the house, where I pause again for a bite of lunch. Then at the post office I dawdle, chatting with a neighbor though wondering at the same time whether I might not be letting the water run too long without checking it down at Reynaldo's squashed culvert. I really don't have a clear idea how long the water takes to get from my place to his over that half to three-quarters of a mile. An hour? Two? By the time I drive down to his place I see I have in fact left it too long: his culvert is completely plugged and water is backing up over the bank and beginning to run down his driveway toward his field. Reynaldo runs down the hill from his house above the ditch and shouts, "I just got home," as I jump out of my truck. Apologetically, as if this is his fault, not mine. The branches and twigs are jammed so tightly into the mouth of the metal culvert that there is no fishing or prying them out with the pitchfork. I get down on hands and knees, roll up my sleeves, grope around in the cold, foamy, muddy water and pull out an assortment of sticks. This is no time to flood a farmer's field, just as he is about to start plowing. Even if I drive up to the lower *desagüe* and shut off the water again— again!—it would still flow down here at full tilt for another couple of hours. Like a freight train, a ditch cannot be stopped at once, particularly at the bottom end. But some small piece of driftwood proves to be the keystone of this underwater construction. With a sigh and a sucking inhalation the blockage disappears into the culvert and belches out the other end, and the water swirls away from the top of the bank and plunges through on its way down a series of cascades toward Porfirio's place, and from there back into the Rio de la Junta.

The ditch is running again its full length, two miles or so, through the back yards of its thirty *parciantes,* through their fields, behind their houses and sheds, past their abandoned cars and trucks, pigpens and chicken coops, under the highway, under arroyos, driveways. People will be thinking about irrigating their alfalfa fields and orchards soon and planting peas and lettuce, carrots, beets, spinach, and reseeding their pastures. And somewhere in the thickets of the Gregory Serna place a muskrat couple is rejoicing again at the water dribbling through the ceiling of their living quarters, and they are planning to expand their burrow, and indeed they may already be at work extending and widening a new tunnel down from the side of the ditch, down through a forest of roots to another smaller hole in the side of the bank a few feet below the channel, their outlet, their *desagüe,* in the soft fragrant clay. . . .

Five

During normal years—if there is such a thing as a normal year—the ditch is usually easy to take care of once the digging is done. But this will be a flood year much like the past two, and if they are any guide we will have a couple of months of the river running high and muddy, and during that time I will have to make a weekly hike down through Harold Castillo's orchard to fish out branches and driftwood from the mouth of the *desagüe* culvert. Rising through March and April, the river will crest in late May or early June, depending on the spring rains, and fill a channel roughly fifty to seventy feet wide with a rushing flow of muddy, turbulent water from three to six feet deep and moving perhaps ten miles an hour, and then can drop rapidly through July to almost nothing in mid-August. Well before the crest our dam of rocks and gravel, sandbags, sheets of

plastic, old roofing tin, branches of cottonwood, juniper will be swept away and we'll have to hire a backhoe in June to build a replacement, which is likely to hold in place the rest of the irrigation season. Then everything will be fine the rest of the summer, providing the late summer or early autumn rains arrive on schedule. Often, of course, they don't.

While the water is running high I don't expect my weekly trips up to the dam to be onerous, particularly if I allow myself time enough to deal with the unforeseen. The section of the ditch I am most attentive to runs about thirty yards from the dam or what is left of it to the *desagüe,* through the thirty-inch culvert, then another hundred yards to Rupert Castillo's place where the channel begins a rapid descent toward the lower *desagüe* a quarter of a mile on. It is crucial to keep these hundred and some yards of ditch running swiftly and the debris cleared out; otherwise the flood will use this stretch as a dumping ground for gravel, sand, and silt, stratified from bottom to top in that order, raising the bottom of the channel in such a way that when the flood ebbs we can find ourselves without water much earlier than usual.

Also out of wariness I customarily hike down through the grass and over two fences to check on Rupert Castillo's field. Last year during spring flood, while searching for water we were losing between the upper and lower *desagües,* I came up against an interesting problem just down from his head gate in the

form of a sodden log three feet long and a foot in diameter, jammed up against some rocks across the
ditch. Laboriously, I pried the log out with my shovel
and dragged it up on the bank. At the time, I thought
its presence in the ditch had caused the water to overflow the low bank and carve a channel back toward
the river, and the log was of the sort you'd expect the
flood to sluice down into the ditch. The channel has a
good slope along there: with the log removed and the
rocks pushed aside, water no longer overflowed the
low bank. But a few days later, the same phenome-
non: lots of water at the upper *desagüe,* very little at
the lower. Again I hiked the whole length, crossing a
half-dozen barbed-wire fences in search of what I
imagined to be some new problem along the most in-
accessible stretch of the ditch. To my surprise, I found
the same log and the same rocks right back where
they had been, but now the overflow channel was
much enlarged and with the curved marks of a shovel
blade sliced into the mud. Behind this annoying business I wondered if there might be some naïve scheme
to turn unirrigated public land into irrigated private
land, with this little diversion being the first step.

I also suspected Rupert Castillo of being the of-
fender. He is an elementary teacher in town and is
locally considered to be particularly difficult in his
dealings with the two or three *acequias* he uses. The
land he farms on our ditch, the only piece that lies to
the north of the channel, he rents from a man who

lives in Utah and whose brother sold us the land on which my wife and I began building our house sixteen years ago. A hundred and fifty yards down from the *presa* and the only property our ditch serves between the *presa* and Ignacio Serna's place a half-mile below, Rupert's rented field probably ought not to be on our ditch at all. Past *mayordomos* have told me that it was put on our rolls when the owner's father or grandfather became *mayordomo* and was led by a quarrel to abandon a middle position on the Los Cerritos ditch in favor of a choice position as first *parciante* on ours. I can't imagine the other *parciantes* lower down having been very happy over the change. At any rate, Rupert has rented the field for several years, growing chile and alfalfa on it. I have never had any trouble with him before the incident with the log, although his dozen Charolais cattle were once famous for their skill in breaking through fences by hooking horns under the wire, lifting their heads and thereby popping staples out of fenceposts, and stepping on through into greener pastures, as I once observed them doing on the way into my place; and as they foraged up and down the valley each winter Rupert's herd generally came to be regarded as his alter ego by those property owners who unwillingly kept it in pasture. And once, some years ago, I was part of a delegation of commissioners from several ditches who had an appointment to meet him at his house early one morning on some inter-ditch business, but which never took place because he refused to come out. Unbeknownst to him, his growling voice carried through the thin walls of his mobile home as we waited patiently outside, the driver now and then taping the horn, until we gave up and drove away.

There is always at least one *parciante* on each ditch who manages to make for himself a reputation of being impossible to deal with, and though my experience with Rupert through the business of the cows and the failed meeting was minor, I put off what I knew was likely to be an unpleasant encounter and instead asked the commission to order him not to irrigate until the business of the log had been discussed. Of course I had not seen Rupert actually put the log into the ditch. And in the past, along that isolated stretch of the ditch, two other Los Cerritos landowners had illicitly pumped and diverted water. But my injunction, which the commission eventually conveyed to Rupert, had the unintended effect of what I suppose you would call entrapment, and I caught him irrigating a month or so later without his having asked my permission, and I took the opportunity to confront him with the business of the log.

Rupert is a short, stocky man in his mid-forties, with black hair and a drooping black moustache, coal-dark eyes, and a broad, strong jaw. He was working shirtless in the sun that day, and the season had already burned a reddish dark tan into his skin. As I climbed the fence and trudged over to where he was standing at the edge of the field, he must have seen that I was grim and determined about something. I asked him right off whether he knew he was not supposed to be irrigating—and since I had jumped into it feet first, whether he was the one who had dumped that log into the ditch twice the month before. A quick and surprised and innocent-seeming "no" was followed by a silence perhaps equally difficult for both of us and then ended in a reluctant correction: "Well, yes, I did, as a matter of fact, come to think of it." He then explained in his hoarse, nasal voice, which carried a trace of irritation or impatience to it, that he had blocked the ditch in order to divert some of the water to the bottomland field he was thinking of buying from the owner in Utah: there seemed to be so much water that he saw no harm in taking a little. I replied that he ought to know that a ditch should never be blocked like that, and as a result of the trouble the log had caused me, I was going to have to ask him to request water the rest of the season every time he wanted to irrigate. This is common procedure, in fact, with the larger ditches across the river; it gives the *mayordomo* some control over the numerous *parciantes,* which in a smaller ditch is normally not needed. Lastly, I told him I was going to ask the commission to levy a fine against the Utah owner of the place, who was unfortunately responsible for whatever Rupert did as tenant.

We parted on reasonable—though not what I would

call friendly—terms, without the insults or threats such encounters can so easily generate. Perhaps the presence of his wife hand-weeding ten yards away throughout our brief conversation quieted in him an urge to argue me down any more than to maintain that his actions were a result of poor judgment, not malice. The nonsense would stop and there wouldn't be a quarrel or a feud, and at my recommendation the commission later levied a fine of twenty dollars, enough to make a point, and which would be talked about in the valley and perhaps induce other water hogs to mend their ways. A month later, the Utah landlord came to the house all very apologetic. Rupert, to his credit, dutifully telephoned me the rest of the season every time he wanted water, which I gave him permission to use without delay; and in the fall I released him from the requirement as long as he could keep his water use reasonable.

The river crests the first week in May and then the weather turns cool, slowing the melting of the mountain snows, and by midmonth the water level has begun to drop. On my weekly inspection trip up to the ditch, I find the beavers have felled another cottonwood over the ditch, but once again it has arched clear of the water. Bad luck again—for the beavers. And the culvert is again clogged with twigs and branches, easy enough to fish out with a rake, and after doing that I follow the renewed surge of water down the ditch bank toward Rupert Castillo's field in search of other obstructions. José Castillo and his wife and daughter are shuffling in a row across the bare earth of their field, one digging a hole with a hoe, the second dropping a seed, the last covering the seed, in a slow, ancient dance. This late in the month it would be beans or possibly sweet corn. A little further down, Rupert's ditch gate is open, diverting a third of the water to his alfalfa, and I wonder how long he has been irrigating. I turn back. A killdeer invites me to its sandbar, where the river turns away to the south along here, trying to lure me from its nest whose location lies in some improbable place in relation to its feinting runs and high, sad seashore cries. They are handsome birds with grey and tan markings on wings and back and a white underbelly, and as they run about on long legs their darting beaks suggest great determination. Several years ago, in the spring, a pair misinterpreted my weeklong absence from a chile field across the river and built a nest on a ridge between two irrigation furrows on sandy, pebbly ground. Perhaps they reasoned, in their way, that no human being would attempt to grow a crop on such land. I discovered the speckled grey-green and black eggs while cultivating with the tractor, just in time not to ruin the unadorned nest. And later, every time I took the tractor over to cultivate I was treated to wonderful displays of simulated broken wings and legs and the song of their piercing, desperate chorus. Toward the

end of the incubation period the hen finally held her
ground and sat silent and quivering on the nest as I
drove the noisy Diesel to within a couple of feet of
her, having decided that the relative quickness of tractor cultivation in the area of the nest would be less
nerve-wracking for all of us than slower work with a
hoe. The last time I cultivated was only a few days
before the chicks hatched, and she stared up at me
with wide liquid eyes fringed in delicately marked
feathers—as I chugged past, staring down at her in
wonder and fear of another kind. I was to glimpse the
chicks only briefly before the mother made them
vanish before my eyes, within arm's reach, when I
came across the new family while checking out the
field on foot: they turned themselves into pebbles and
shadows in a flash, and I was never to see them again.

I walk back up to the dam and then back up through
Harold Castillo's orchard to the truck and then drive
down to the lower *desagüe* where I clean branches out
of the gates, and then drive over to my makeshift
grate at the siphon next to the highway to fish more
debris out of its re-bar teeth. In flood the water first
turns a muddy coffee-and-cream brown as the reddish clay of the lower elevation banks is torn away,
then goes a smokier brown as the river crests, bringing down the dark earth of the high mountain streams
and sending the forest's fragile humus down through
the valley toward the Gulf of Mexico. Some communities regard the silt-laden floodwaters as rich in nu-

trients, but ours takes the opposite view, that they are bad for fields and crops, a view I do not at all share: I'm quite happy to see the muddy water flow down my rows, building up the soil.

We stare out the windows in disbelief. A spring hailstorm, a rare occurrence heareabouts, is stripping the leaves from the trees and pulping the petunias I set out only this morning, and flattening the vegetable garden which at last is—or was—beginning to show some rapid growth. The time is three in the afternoon, Monday, May nineteenth. Will the hail take the fruit off the trees? The apples? The peaches? The plums? Will it ruin our acre of garlic? A half-hour seems to drag by, though the reality may only have been ten minutes. The ground is covered with hailstones the size of thumbtacks. I pick up a book, try to read. I don't want to go outside. Nature rarely produces ugly effects, but this will be one of them. Later, during dinner, the phone rings. A kid, a boy, Horacio Vasques's ten-year-old son Jimmy says the ditch is plugged up, could I please come. Plugged up with hailstones?—I wonder as my son and I throw shovels, a rake, a pitchfork into the back of the truck. And why aren't they unplugging it themselves?—something else I failed to ask Jimmy. Five minutes later, driving up the bumpy dirt road that serves as a driveway to Horacio's and his brother Reynaldo Vasques's places, we are greeted by a stream of muddy water already carving a small ditch into the roadway, while to the left, below, water is advancing into Reynaldo's field. It turns out that the culvert under his driveway is jammed not with hailstones but with the usual storm-dislodged debris of leaves and branches, packed into the constricted sheet-metal mouth by the force of muddy water surging down the steep drop into it. Neither rake nor pitchfork is strong enough to free anything. I throw tools aside and drop to my hands and knees and thrust my hands into the opaque water, something I seem to remember having done here not long ago. If I can't unblock the culvert Reynaldo's field will be ruined for planting, if he hasn't already planted, or simply ruined—seeds washed away, irrigation rows silted up, beds caved in, if this much water pours into it much longer. He and his brother Horacio must both be away in town somewhere. Most of the branches are so tightly jammed I can't pull them out. But then somehow I am in luck. The keystone of this construction, invisible deep under the surface, turns out to be a stubby piece of gnarled driftwood, and the moment I pull it out a bolus of branches and tumbleweeds is driven through the culvert to shoot out the other end. A rich sucking sound announces that the culvert will now draw. The water level begins to lower and soon declines below the bank. We throw the tools back into the truck and before leaving I instruct Jimmy, still excited at the earlier promise of catastrophe, on how to unplug a culvert. Less work, on the whole, than run-

111

ning upriver across three muddy fields to the nearest telephone, which is what he did to call me. But he is a nice kid. And at least he did something. But then, on reflection, a kid might risk being sucked into the mouth of the two-foot-wide culvert when it begins to draw again, a thoroughly frightening prospect. Perhaps, after all, what he did was just the right thing.

Jimmy is Horacio's youngest son. We have supplied him and his teen-age sisters with several generations of kittens, and they are always anxious to report on the stages of their pets' lives and their then abrupt deaths in feline middle age. I am probably one of the few people with whom Horacio Vasques, his father, speaks English. He has a hoarse, gasping way of exhaling his repertory of English phrases, always responding to my "*¿Cómo está?*" with a "No very good," a quavering hold on the "good." He is Reynaldo's older brother. One would guess him to be well over eighty, though he says he is not quite seventy. He has always answered my queries for some ten years now in much the same way, "No feeling very good," with a wide grin that brings out the angular boyishness of his face. Now and then while I furrow his field each spring with my tractor, an old woman in long cotton skirts comes and goes through the back door of their cement-plastered but unpainted adobe on some errand to the trash barrel or clothesline. Horacio Vasques is the third from the last on the ditch, always pays cash punctually as soon as it is due or in installments when he's short of money. When I was treasurer, owing the ditch money seemed a positive agony to him. Of the people I know in the valley his life is perhaps closest to what it used to be for most inhabitants in the old days, a life of self-sufficiency in food from a couple of acres of land, a dozen fruit trees, a few pigs. No phone, no tractor, and because he has given up his team of draft horses he must ask his neighbors and relations to plow and furrow his productive one-acre garden, and he lets his brother or another relation farm the lower field. He is up to date only in the inordinate amount of time he seems to spend in his well-kept but aging car and truck, driving back and forth to town hunched over the wheel, face pressed forward almost to the glass.

After a couple of weeks the tattered fields and orchards begin to show signs of recovering, and in the first week of June the days become hot and dry, good growing weather coming a little earlier than usual. *Parciantes* all up and down the ditch will suddenly want to irrigate at once in this kind of weather. The first Tuesday of June, I drive up to check the dam and then walk down to Rupert's, where I find he has turned a third of the ditch on to his spongy alfalfa patch. I wonder how long he has had the water running here but decide to wait until the end of the week to come back and check again, and if he's still taking that much water on Friday I'll give him a call.

As I turn away from his field there's a whitish flash

113

down in the ditch, right below me. Trout? Rat? I freeze. Through here, the ditch carves its way below ground level like a gully through a rise of higher ground covered in grasses and a thin stand of young cottonwoods, survivors of a fire several years ago, an area bordering both Rupert's and José Castillo's fields on the south. The rise, in fact, allows Rupert's field to be irrigated from our ditch while lying on what, elsewhere except this one spot, is the uphill side. A ring of blackened stones amid the cottonwoods marks the site of summer campfires where kids from Los Cerritos probably now and then hike down for full-moon drinking bouts. After a minute or so, out of the grass growing down the side of the bank into the water there emerges the blunt snout of some creature, nose twitching. Beady black eyes next appear—yet trusting, wide, like those of a mouse. A muskrat. It stares me in the eye—seemingly. I remain frozen. We are about eight feet from each other. It decides I am something else. Post. Tree. Laundry. It starts crawling out into a stretch of the ditch channel where there is no longer a protective drapery of grasses, bearing in its mouth a sprig of alfalfa no doubt taken from Rupert's field. Good fellow. Help yourself to as much as you like. The round roly-poly body is almost a foot long, with wet brown fur fading toward tan over a darker undercoat, and a long black or dark brown tail, smooth and hairless, longer perhaps than the body. The muskrat passes slowly out of sight beneath a clump of grass growing out of the bank, possibly toward its burrow. Along here it may dig away with no danger to the ditch, and in fact its excavations may help widen and deepen the channel across the high ground and thus to improve the flow. I wait for it to reappear, but perhaps it has reached its burrow or a relatively secure place where it can wait for me to go about my business. It may have seen me and then pretended not to, or has caught my scents of coffee, motor oil, leather. In fact it may have come to know quite a bit about me over the years of watching me come and go to this place, much more than I know about it. The muskrat may even know what I am likely to do next: lose interest, walk away, noisy as a horse or cow.

I walk back up to the truck and drive down to the lower *desagüe* where I increase the flow to the maximum of the limiter board, raising it to the lowermost of the four ranks of nails that serve as stops. But the hot day turns out to have been preparing itself for a good heavy rain through the night—unusual for this time of year. The ditch holds, but in a drizzle at noon the next day, worried that the river will rise, I walk up from the highway through Leandro Castillo's place and drop the limiter board back down to the lowest setting, reducing the flow by half into the ditch. On my way back I clean out the grate at the siphon as best I can with my shovel. An aerosol can, label worn off its bright metal, dings against the corrugated steel walls of the siphon and swirls around in the muddy water in the company of white styrofoam shards—of what, a cup?

A week later, in mid-June, I return home hot and tired from Santa Fe to an empty house. A fresh breezy morning has become a muggy afternoon. I doze off on the couch around three. I am almost immediately awakened, or so it seems, by distant cries and shrieks, the barking of dogs, what I guess to be a party of children down at the river. The river runs by our place at the foot of our drive, a hundred and fifty yards from the house. It is early for kids to be in the water. The water is cold and the river is still running high, and though the sounds that have echoed up from the river before have never meant anything more than children having a noisy good time over the years, I am still apprehensive. My day in town has been one of odd sounds and near accidents—a pinging, metallic ricocheting noise too close to an open window, the coming upon a motorcycle accident on Cerrillos Road where an old man bends over to pick a helmet up off the pavement. His son's? Does the kid lie dead in an ambulance parked up against the median of the four-lane thoroughfare? Then, later, a semi passing on a curve near home, gravel spraying out over the top of its bed and splashing across the windshield, yet miraculously not marking it. A day of near misses.

The cries and screams of what I now understand to

be probably inner-tubers rapidly grow faint to the west, downriver, and then cease. They have come and gone with a speed which does little to reassure me: the river could be moving at close to ten miles an hour along rocky, brushy banks that would make it impossible for anyone on foot to keep up with them—to imagine the worst, that they are in distress. Or am I just spooked by the hints of the day? They could have been the cries of high spirits and excitement in the still-cold water, nothing more. The muggy afternoon remains silent beyond the low roar of the distant river, which can be heard through a screen of cottonwoods and willows lining its banks. After a while I make myself some coffee. In the distance, as the water comes to a boil, there slowly rises the wailing of a siren through the valley, upriver, and then back down closer, down the dirt road toward our house, along the river. I pour the coffee but leave it untouched. The tires are still hard on the old bicycle I sometimes use to check the irrigation at the Thompson place, where we grow garlic; I don't want to block the narrow road with the truck if this is the emergency the day with its ambiguous signals has been preparing to announce. I pedal down the dirt road set back some twenty or thirty yards from the winding river course and a quarter of a mile down come across the volunteer fire department ambulance parked with its nose in a clump of willows. Further down the road, near the cattleguard at Wilfred and Virginia Ortiz's place stands Fritz Wetzel, a retired Soil Conservation Service man and mainstay of the fire department, who is waiting to give directions to the rest of the crew as it arrives. What he has heard is that two kids of a party of four inner-tubers fell into the water, and one got out and the other has disappeared. The rest of the day and into the night a traffic of State Police cars and vehicles of relatives and friends of the missing kid plus the usual curiosity seekers drive up and down the dead-end road late into the night. The missing kid, a twelve-year-old boy, Mark Espinosa, whom my kids remember from their time at the local school, lives somewhere across the river from us. Over the next day the story emerges. The inner-tubers had all got out of the water several places downriver from ours, which apparently they passed without difficulty, but at the bend where they got out Mark Espinosa slipped back into the current while they were all trying to free an inner tube snagged on the barbed wire of a fence downed by the floodwaters. He disappeared under swirling water perhaps ten feet deep at a log jam, a place where the river's headlong rush, momentarily checked, whirlpooled around a deep hole. They never saw him again.

Through the afternoon and into the night and beyond, the whereabouts of the missing kid comes to preoccupy everyone in the valley. Everyone becomes obsessed by the events of the day, tracing and retracing the steps and decisions that led the four kids to launch their inherently dangerous craft into the fatally swift river too early in the season—as a kayaker had done up in the box canyon the year before, drowning when trapped between boulders. The next morning at six, Juliana Espinosa, *mayordoma* of the Acequia de las Juntas, telephones me to suggest that if we all put as much water as we can into our ditches, then the river will lower, making it easier for the State Police divers to find the body. Juliana is related by marriage to the boy, and only last year her own eldest son was killed while felling a cottonwood tree next to her house. This new grief must unbearably sharpen the old. But there is enough water roaring down the river for twenty or thirty ditches. I don't tell her I am skeptical. Yet after getting my two field workers into the garlic rows at seven-thirty that morning, I drive up to the lower *desagüe* and raise the limiter board to its highest setting, more out of superstition than the belief that anything anyone can now do in this way can actually help. On my way home I rake out the debris from the grate at the siphon: aerosol can and styrofoam shards still float in its swirling maw.

Later that day, all afternoon: the sound of a bulldozer trying to move the river channel away from the hole where the divers in black rubber suits think the body may be snagged. But the water is too swift, the rechanneling fails.

A week later they find the body in a reservoir sixty miles downstream.

Six

On the north side of the river, in the bottomlands of La Jara, the cold air tends to pool and can often produce a frost even after a hot clear day, particularly on the heels of a storm. Only by mid-June is it finally safe to put out tomatoes and other tender plants. By then also late-planted winter squash and hard-shell gourds will break through the crust of earth at last, and the last days of the month will end in a race with weeds in fields and gardens—often to be lost at either or both ends of vegetable rows, in tangles of wild grasses and alfalfa and clover suddenly grown waist high. At this time in the summer the garden or field planted to row crops will seem less a whole than a series of disjointed parts, each crying out for individual attention: more water here, less there, fertilizer in this corner, cultivation here, but weeds, always weeds, seedling and full grown, everywhere. For a week the ditch mercifully calls for no attention at all, the weather settles, the river lowers, and when on June twentieth I drive up to the dam to see how things are going I find that the river has assumed its summer look and coloration, water faintly greenish or olive-tinged as the algae begin to grow on the rocks beneath the surface. As I peer down into the narrow pond at the mouth of the culvert, an eight-inch trout wriggles in place and then shoots upstream. The river is now thirty to forty feet wide, perhaps two to three feet deep at the center, still a lot of water flowing by, still possibly dangerous to the imprudent. The killdeer couple, a flock of blackbirds, a few magpies object to my presence. I wonder how the killdeer fool the magpies, eaters of chicken and duck eggs, nest robbers, killers of goslings down on which they swoop under the noses of the ponderous parents, peck to death, drag off. The lowering water level in the ditch tells me I must trade my rake for a shovel next time I come up here, and then, a week or two later, mid-July, summon a work crew or a backhoe. The spring flood has carried away the dam. Nothing remains of it except a couple of submerged boulders.

Later, at the lower *desagüe,* which is now ringed by a lush growth of ragweed and willows, the scent of spearmint—the native mint, a pale green variety— wafts from underfoot. I must dig up a plant someday for the garden. And next trip up here I need to bring a sheet of black plastic, some two-by-fours, and a saw. A couple of the splashboards need replacing. I lay some more rocks on top of the stone dike, building it up. Next time I will seal it with plastic.

At the siphon, the same scene: aerosol can, styrofoam shards. I clean the re-bar teeth with my rake, pull out leaves, twigs, small branches. A fat tomato worm perches on a branch of my growing pile of debris on the north bank of the ditch, next to the mouth of the siphon. It's an unhealthy yellow color, the worm, not the usual pea-green, and barely moves at my prodding. Diseased, probably; I leave it undisturbed.

By July the flooding river has swept itself downstream to leave a quieter, clearer flow, and the memory of that other begins to fade, to offer the possibility that it might have been only a nightmare; another river has taken its place, a gentler mountain stream that seems unrelated to its torrential parent, clear now, not murky, murmuring and splashing, not roaring and booming, a stream that will soon let itself be walked across even by children. We are seven working on the banks and in the water up at the dam on the morning of the third of July, a bright clear day; the water is just warm enough now to wade and swim in without numbness, and knowing we would have to get wet I asked the crew to meet at ten rather than eight. The Serrano clan has come this morning, Orlando with his chainsaw, his seventy-year-old brother Ewaldo, their fifteen-year-old nephew Steve, and Lauriano Serna who has come to work off his substantial *delincuencias* and Irwin Serna putting in for his uncle Gregory, and my son, whom I have asked to work for the Thompson place we rent and are not exempt for.

We are here to put some more water into the ditch as there have been delays in getting a backhoe down from a village ten miles up the mountain from us; though there's still plenty of water in the river, the flood scoured out a deeper channel and threw up a roll of gravel and rocks into the mouth of the ditch, and now very little water is entering. Everyone knows what to do without being told. Ewaldo has probably built and repaired dams for our ditch fifty or sixty times in his life, perhaps more, and everyone else here (except myself) has done this work since the time they were kids. A large cottonwood rotten at the base has fallen conveniently over the mouth of the ditch, and Orlando sets about cutting up the limbs to man-ageable length, to drag out into the water. Forty-five-year-old Lauriano Serna, black-bearded and bearlike in shorts and sneakers and free this day of the arthritis he has complained of ever since I have known him, moves out into the water with the younger men and boys to begin lifting and rolling rocks into a line against which branches and logs can be buttressed. Then a couple of the boys wade across the river, no more than knee-deep now, and walk up to a sandbar where some logs have beached and drag and roll them into the water and launch them down toward the dam. The bright morning grows rapidly hot and the nip of the water turns refreshing. The work progresses rapidly. Five feet at a time the crew extends the fragile barrier out into the flow, securing logs with rocks, chinking gaps with twigs and branches cut from nearby willows and junipers and held in place with more rocks, all the while laughing and shouting, cracking jokes, shouting out commands and requests for more logs and rocks and brush. The moment is luminous and transparent: boys and men working together in the dancing reflections of the water to build that most essential structure, the beaver dam. And at this sweeping bend in the river course overhung by clumps of cottonwood and a clear blue sky, with the still slanting sunlight on the glaring white ribbons of sand and bleached rocks along the banks, we work to the alpine sounds of rushing water and the clacking of rocks smashing against each other, the plaintive and spasmodic whine of the saw, the shouts and laughter, the rustle and splash of boughs being thrown and dragged into the water; for this moment men become boys again and boys at last become men, as they assemble piecemeal what backhoes and bulldozers with their powerful blades and buckets can do so much better—yet, in another sense, can never do at all. And later perhaps we will remember only that we built a beaver dam to bring water to our gardens, in the way people have built them all over the world for thousands of years, and that we came home wet and aching and satisfied far beyond what we could easily explain to those who weren't there.

After an hour's work we have a good flow into the ditch and can count on it running full for a few days at least, perhaps even a week. The river, like the mountain rains, is unpredictable in early summer, and though the upper valleys may be sending more water downstream while drying out fields for the first cutting of hay, the six *acequias* immediately upriver from us may also soon tighten up their dams to let even less water flow past, in the manner we have just done with ours. Yet we should be safe for a couple of days. Before dismissing the crew I have the men plug up some holes around the culvert at the *desagüe* with clumps of grass and mud. Then I drive on down to the lower *desagüe* and find that we have done well indeed: there is more water here than the crumbling cement structure can hold, and perhaps a third of the flow is sloshing over the bank back to the river. I set the limiter board at its highest mark, sending a swift, clear flow rushing down the ditch and raising high the grasses skirting the banks, water chirping throatily. After days of a low and desultory flow, to see the banks full again is especially gratifying, and for the moment there is no risk in running the ditch full to the brim since *parciantes* all up and down will be drawing water off to irrigate day and night. On my way home, I stop at the siphon to clean weeds out of the grate. The aerosol can bangs away less musically now, perhaps from having taken on water, and the white styrofoam shards have been worn down to the size of quarters.

Our handmade dam is too porous to serve for long if the river continues to lower and too fragile to survive even a small flood, so when Marcos Roybal from up the hill gives me a time when he can bring his backhoe down a week later I tell him to go ahead. He rebuilt our dam last year at this time, an elegant serpentine of rocks and gravel that reached halfway out across the river channel to broach the current in such a way that as the water level lowered the flow tended to move to the left or north of the dike, thus into the ditch, while in flash floods the current rode over the dike and moved to the right or south side and remained in the main channel as it curves away toward the southwest. It takes Roybal five hours to replace the dam one afternoon in mid-July, and after inspecting his always careful work I meet him at Ignacio Serna's, where he has parked his dump truck and trailer, and hand him over an *acequia* check for $120 plus a five-dollar bill. The treasury of the Acequia de la Jara is now down to about $3. I apologize for the fact that last year's check bounced (it was immediately made good) and tell him that I hope it won't happen again. Roybal is a burly, slow-speaking fellow of thirty-five, reserved and courteous; he smiles at my remark and says: "No problem."

At noon on Friday, the nineteenth of July, the phone rings. Over the receiver comes the breathy voice of Reynaldo Vasques, next to the last man on the ditch, which can only mean one thing. Usually he has one of his relatives more articulate in English call me, one of his sons or sons-in-law, whose message, as if recorded, cannot be negotiated: My father (or father-in-law) needs the water this very minute. Over the years, I have come to think of Reynaldo as growing especially sensitive varieties of corn and chile which are never able to recover from their first signs of stress or wilting. Now Reynaldo and I exchange politenesses for a few moments while I adjust to the idea of having to go chase after water this afternoon. The ditch has gone down abruptly in the past two days, I know, down to half what it was, even though the river seems little changed. I was going to check the *desagües* and the dam yesterday, but it was too hot and I was tired and overworked, or was it the day before?

"I need water," he says, with the hoarse, scratchy voice of one well practiced in the theatrics of the request. "There's only a little bit down here."

"When do you need it, Reynaldo?" An unnecessary question. I know when he needs it: right now.

"I'm irrigating and I don't have enough for even

one row." Wonderful quavering emphasis on the last phrase.

"I'll get you some water by this afternoon," I hear myself saying. "I'm irrigating myself at the Thompson's is part of the problem. But I should finish up sometime this afternoon." And I add that I'll check the dam. This is picking day, and besides finishing my irrigation I should be packing the truck for the farmers' market tomorrow. I wonder how I'll find the time and energy to do anything else.

When? Right now. Then it will be done. I'll check the lower *desagüe* first on the chance there's an obstruction there, which would also save me a trip to the dam and that long hot walk down through Harold Castillo's orchard and back up to the truck. And at Nick Manzanares's place, before I even get out of the truck I can see the ditch is brimming with water as it winds its way along the shady edge of Nick's lawn, and soon I can hear it splashing through the distant *desagüe* back toward the river. There's more than enough water here. At the *desagüe* the flow under the limiter board is slow and glassy. Somewhere beyond the leaning cottonwood there must be an obstruction. I climb the fence and clamber up into Gerald López's pasture, take a shortcut across it toward where the ditch passes back under the fence, to run inside the field, where I notice that a large cottonwood has been recently felled by beavers parallel to the ditch, right next to it. I am told their aim is not very good: perhaps what they depend on is the fact that a majority of trees lining river courses tend to lean over the water anyway. Yet with branches chewed off the tree the beavers have built a dam right in the ditch, a dam which chokes off most of the flow and backs the water up into the *desagüe,* where it spills back into the river. Expecting to get wet I have worn old tennis shoes and shorts. I climb down into the water, refreshingly cool at least, and set to pulling out branches. The key branch turns out to be a juniper limb the beavers have trimmed off a nearby tree. As I pile the branches up on the bank I wonder if the animals won't just drag them back into the water. Is there one beaver or are there two? And might not it—or they—be inside here, in this thicket of sodden twigs and branches, ready to defend the structure with what I imagine to be very large and sharp teeth? Some of the branches slip from my grasp, sweep downstream past my legs. I climb out of the water and run down the bank and hook what I can with my shovel.

The water has drained from my tennis shoes by the time I walk back to the truck. I climb inside the hot cab and drive back up the long driveway to the Los Cerritos road and then down the highway to the siphon, whose re-bar grate is bending under the pressure of the water dammed up behind it by the leafy remnants of the beavers' construction. I climb down into the water, tug out the branches and twigs and a Budweiser carton in bright red and pale blue, unleashing a deluge that fills the mouth of the siphon and promises briefly to take the seemingly indestructible aerosol can down into its depths.

There often comes a time in summer around mid-August when a peculiar reversal can take place in my relations to fields and crops, a moment when I feel myself having become an almost unconscious instrument of that which I am more accustomed to thinking myself in control of. By this time, when the days are long and hot, in a calculating and keeping-track-of sense I have given up trying to remain conscious of the amazing multiplicity of growth that has arisen from nothing to spread out over the five or six acres under my guidance: I have no time to think about it anymore, I must simply race to keep up with it all and to maintain and hold it in that less critical area of the mind where so much of the world resides as a jumble of images and sensations and memories whose meaning in some logical or coherent sense has come to seem pointless or irrelevant to the demands of action. From then on I cease planning and simply spend as much time in my fields as I can in order to remain alert to their needs, to work for them according to their barrages of subtle hints and instructions. If I am not quite at one with my rows of corn, chile, tomatoes, onions, the white-blossoming buckwheat, or with the dust and the water, rain, the river, rocks, gravel, the swarms of insects, then I do not feel entirely distinguishable from them either, and they are much of what I am; and the distances I skipped over rapidly while walking in the winter become in summer like miles, like the distances small creatures must overcome, so many times must I traverse them to irrigate, cultivate, harvest; and all of that which I now only dimly remember having planted—the result, oddly it seems now, of former plans, intentions, histories—and the distances and weights and time and space itself undergo the distortions of the new terms under which I labor, and the faces I live amongst are the fruit of vines, their flowers, the swelling shapes on stalks, the grim expression of a stone that is always in the way in a field, trees, bushes, clumps of orchard grass, dead branches along a ditch, the glare of a shovel blade polished by hours of digging, and those mechanical faces, grill and headlights of tractor or truck, always patiently awaiting me at the edge of a field. Human faces become too quick and impatient and mocking for my field-possessed self, too cruel, too cutting for the fatigue that is the claim my fields have staked in my body, those fields within me that I dream of and rest in relation to and am always going to or coming from, the fields that live in me like the presence of a wife or child. But in all this I am also relieved in what seems to be an honest and forthright way of that burdensome and complaining and spoiled self with its desperately important habits and preferences and its weaknesses and susceptibility to all the toys and trash the industrial world can think up, its schemings for privilege and power, and its thirst above all to be relieved of its own individualistic curses: all this goes, sometimes wholly, but often only fleetingly, in August when the fields have reached a pitch of growth and leaves can grow no larger or vines no longer, as they strain to capture and hold the high blazing light.

A change will come soon. The light will shift. From the abundant, effulgent vegetation the plants will begin to withdraw the reserves they have placed in leaves and stalks and vines, and dispatch them to the seeds and the fruits, and the fields will start to yellow and tatter on their surfaces and edges, and soon there will open up in an angle of changing light the possibility that perhaps very soon all of this will come to an end of one kind or another, either sudden and abrupt in an early frost within a month or less— or, one hopes, in a long and languishing decline toward a snowfall late in October. Consciousness in the form of will, intention, plan timidly begins reappearing, ego resurrects, but now into a world strangely altered, now doomed in this form, even though the days seem just as long and hot, just as impossibly eternal; and from now on, into autumn and winter, I will become haunted by the growing withdrawal of those fields of August as they imperceptibly turn brown and shrivel and die upon their surfaces, give way, in their way, to a kind of forgetfulness. And then

I will await the transformation somewhere within myself that will finally emerge, as soon as I am certain that the days are indeed growing longer, into plans and into the first small plantings of the mind that will eventually again bring out of the earth what will come to seem, in the dead of winter, so hopelessly remote. . . .

Hot, clear afternoons, time pressing, no time to walk down the blazing, dusty driveway to the river or what remains of it now, a few pools, to take a cooling dip, so instead I bound up the bank behind the house and strip off my clothes under the cottonwood and cherry trees and step down into the ditch, so arched over now with hemlock and *oshá* in seed, poison oak, long drooping grasses, that the channel appears to be only half the width of what we cleaned out in the spring, and where now the willows bend again over the water, and milkweed, wild rose and plum and squawberry again crowd the narrow flow hurrying past. There is enough water to immerse myself in, even dip my head under. This is a busy place for life even without my large splashing disruptions. Orb weavers spin their nets across the ditch every yard or so, concessionaires along the liquid highway, water spiders skate the surface, brown-oared beetles row the depths near the edges. The odor is of humus, muck, mud, silt, of decay proceeding in an orderly manner.

Mayordomo

By late August the river is mostly bones, its rocks protruding from the water and the brownish algae with which they are coated bleaching in the sun. Cottonwoods once lining the water now stand back forlorn at the edge of a glaring desert. Yet there is still enough of a flow to fill the ditch at the dam, but for some reason not much of it is reaching the lower *desagüe*. One hot afternoon I discover a series of obstructions between Rupert's place and the upper *desagüe*: branches, twigs, leaves which I am at first convinced have been thrown into the ditch by a heedless or malicious landowner clearing a field or a fenceline, though as I work away dismantling the first dam I notice the willow and cottonwood twigs I had thought to be cut by a hatchet or machete resemble at their ends the angular slices made by a beaver's teeth. Three such dams within a hundred feet of each other, ten minutes each to clear them out by standing in the water and pulling them apart with bare hands—and soon I am too winded and sweaty to care much about the agency of the mess. I hike down the ditch past Rupert's and through three or four fences, across the tall scratchy grass, halfway down to the lower *desagüe* in search of more obstructions, but find none and turn back. On my way, almost back to the upper *desagüe,* I understand the meaning of something I saw before: a bare patch of earth worn through the grass on the top of the ditch bank, a foot-wide saddle of bare earth such as would

135

be made, I now realize, by an animal crawling in and out of the ditch again and again. A few feet below the bank, directly in the path, the chewed remains of a cottonwood sapling and on the stump and shavings littering the ground around it and now yellowing in the sun, markings distinctly those of a beaver's teeth.

I walk on up to the dam, wondering if I will have get the commission to buy a long sheet of black plastic to drape over the dike to cut down on the seepage under the rocks, a loss that now equals what flows into the ditch. Aside from when we worked on it in June, before the backhoe came, I have been able to get by so far without having to tighten it up any more. Though I am in no mood to think so at the moment, I know that this can sometimes be refreshing and even entertaining work. Two years ago an Australian doctor friend staying with us on vacation, Alister Brass, hesitantly accepted my invitation one hot August afternoon to go "repair the dam." I was certain he would rather have driven up to the mountains or to a tourist attraction he had not yet visited on his many trips to see us, but I had too many things to do— among which was to get some more water down the ditch. But whenever he could look on the farm work he often helped us with as a kind of healthy recreation like skiing or scuba diving, Alister would become obsessively energetic and devoted to the task at hand and almost unstoppable. Once we had hiked down through Harold's orchard and had waded into the shallow water, he threw himself into the work with great relish. For the next hour or so he staggered about in his bathing trunks carrying fifty-pound rocks and logs as we extended the dam out into the channel, upstream, heaving rocks, shouting, reveling in the crashing splashes. "Never had so much fun in my life," he announced when we were done. Somewhat tongue in cheek I wrote out a *papelito* for two hours' work, worth five dollars at the time. As one who had been almost religiously addressed as "doctor," at least in this country where he spent much of his working life as an editor of medical journals, he was particularly pleased at being described in writing as a "*pión*" and said he was going to have the *papelito* framed for his office back in Sydney.

Later that afternoon, I hike down to the river from the house for a more relaxing dip in one of the few remaining pools opposite Gregory Serna's field. An old cottonwood leans out over the river course here, and you have to scramble down a low but steep bank of stones which can become burning hot in the afternoon sun. I plunge in quickly, and as I sit in the more or less cool water I hear little cries coming from somewhere, high-pitched squeakings of distress of a sort I have never heard before. For a moment I am even uncertain whether they are coming from close or far away, so faint yet intimate are they. The river has eroded into the bank of gravel on the north side along here, the bank I have to climb down into the water, and there are cavities where the rocks and gravel have dropped away into the water, forming very small caves hung with the dangling roots of the nearby cotton-wood and from willows growing atop the bank. An apparition almost within arm's reach startles me. A bat has fallen into the water at the very edge of the gravel bank and lies pinned under a stone the size of a fist only five feet away from where I am now standing up in the water. I find a stick, push off the stone, nudge the creature up out of the water: furry grey head, blondish hairs, a big wide mouth on a flat broad nose. It is like a miniature monkey but with beady mouse-like eyes. It flips itself over and lies face down on the rocks and faintly flutters its wings, apparently still not where it would want to be. But where? This is too much brightness for it, too much heat. With the tip of the stick I snag one of its wing-claws and lift it up into the cave and into the shrublike growth of ex-posed roots, in the shade. The bat easily snags a root with the other claw, releases the stick, hangs itself upside down by both its claws, and now faces me. The creature is clearly pleased and at once sets about grooming itself like a cat, pulling at its fur, arranging itself, ready soon to resume its rudely interrupted sleep. I sink back into the pool, immerse myself up to my neck. Probably what happened was that on my way down the bank my tramping footsteps released some rocks from the roof of the bat's fragile cave and tumbled it down into the water just as I was jumping in myself.

My summer afternoon dips in this source of our
lives do not always inspire the most cheerful reflections, particularly when I am alone and exhausted
and know I will be hard pressed to continue working
through the heat of the afternoon. Immersing myself
in cold water, even only slightly cold, always seems to
me a kind of dying: the air-creature's fear of water
which it knows to be death in sufficient quantity. And
though it is a source of life, a stream or river is also
a sewer, a treatment plant for the natural world in
which decaying matter is broken down and carried
away. Here at the river and often at work in my fields
I have now and then wondered over the years what
it must be like to live in a small community such as
this when it finds itself becoming a battlefield in
one of those wars conducted largely in rural, tropical
places which the United States has had a hand in,
the Vietnams, the El Salvadors, the Nicaraguas, and
what it would be like to be working in a field or
swimming in the river or walking a ditch bank and
find oneself suddenly in the way of an attack of one
sort or another. These are not entirely abstract or
media-inspired reflections. Our narrow little valley is
on the route of twice-monthly training runs of military turboprop transports of the sort the CIA would
use for airlifts; they traverse the valley lengthwise at
an altitude of a thousand feet or less. Not quite as frequently, paired jet fighter-bombers roar across the
hilltops at low altitudes from varying directions, rat-
tling windows and causing panic in henhouses, re-

minding us that the picturesque landscape in which we live may be little different, except in the one fact of its peacefulness, from those the great powers have often chosen for destruction. Nor in fact has our valley been exempted, though the memory is no longer living. A hundred and fifty years ago the village found itself in the path of a young and arrogant nation expanding to the west. In the Battle of La Silla Pass (as I will call it) of 1847, up an arroyo perhaps two miles from where I live, resisting "rebels" suffered twenty dead and sixty wounded in a clash with a detachment of the U.S. Cavalry. The total population of the valley at the time is not known, but the effect in any era of the loss of that much manpower in a small place could have taken generations to recover from. Crosses—*descansos*—chipped into the black basalt boulders of the pass still mark the site of the battle in which this area came to be swallowed up by the United States of America.

Seven

During the month of August the Rio de la Jara has been known to dry up completely in sort stretches along its two and a half mile run through our narrow valley, and particularly in the upper half between the dam of the Acequia de la Jara and those of the two ditches immediately upriver from ours. We have also known equally dry Junes and Octobers, but from about 1970, when I first became a commissioner, until the summer of 1980, our driest year in my time here, August through much of September have proven our most difficult months. Since 1981 we have had a succession of wet years, and most of the ditches have not had to make use of the elaborate procedures by which water is both rationed within a ditch and also by which the river is divided up among seven of the nine ditches. And by late August of this year, 1985, it is apparent that unless the mountains receive no more rain at all we will be able to finish the season without rationing.

In a dry season, however, as soon as there is no longer enough water to go around, the commission will put all of the *parciantes* on a ditch "on hours," which is different from the various forms of scheduling most ditches above a certain size will employ most of the time during the irrigation season. My ditch, the Jara, is usually able to operate without any kind of schedule well into a dry spell, and the first thing we sometimes do is divide the ditch in half, the upper half being from the dam to Wilfred Ortiz's place, the lower half starting at Arthur Litton's, the next place down, and running to the end of the ditch, with each half taking the water about eighty-four hours a week. In theory, going on hours will be the next step. For this, the commission will draw up a weekly schedule assigning irrigation times in chronological order up or down the ditch, starting from one end or the other, which means that many *parciantes* will have to irrigate in the middle of the night or during working hours or at other inconvenient times, although there is always a certain leeway in the arrangement owing to the fact that not all *parciantes* will want to irrigate each week and that a few may be willing to trade hours. Also, unused fields owned by absentee landowners will allow some juggling.

Each *parciante*'s hours will be determined not only by where his property lies on the ditch but also by how many shares or *piones* his property counts as a portion of the whole ditch. The Acequia de la Jara numbers about thirty *parciantes* whose shares range from one-half to two *piones* each, with a total of about thirty *piones* for the whole ditch. Were we to go on hours for one-week periods, each *pión* would be worth about six hours per week (during which time the *parciante* will often have the right to take the whole ditch), which given the small size of most places can hardly be called rationing. However, when the whole river is being divided up between "upper" and "lower" ditches, which I will explain below, our weekly irrigation period shrinks to about ninety hours at best, and each *pión* is entitled to about three hours of water per week, assuming everything works out as planned—which is rarely the case. For a small and easily irrigated field, three hours is adequate; for a larger or more difficult field to be furthermore irrigated in the middle of the night, three hours may fall far short of what is needed. Shares, of course, do not exactly correspond to the size and peculiarities of fields. Also, in order to avoid going on hours we have now and then tried a priority system whereby *parciantes* are asked to irrigate at night orchards and pastures, which can be more easily flooded, but are allowed to irrigate row crops and gardens by day.

In order to go on hours, the commission has to draw up a schedule matching the list of *parciantes'* shares to the time period in question, usually a week.

A longer period risks running afoul of changing weather. Once a schedule is drawn up, the commission or the *mayordomo* writes out *papelitos* for each *parciante,* giving the day and the inclusive hours during which the *parciante* may irrigate; the *mayordomo* then distributes the *papelitos* up and down the ditch. The *parciante* can also telephone in for his or her hours (supposing the *mayordomo* has a phone), but in really difficult times it is considered prudent for each *parciante* to have in hand a *papelito*—in order to resolve disputes, correct errors, or to assure that the commission is assigning hours in an equitable manner. Since customs vary widely from area to area, what I am reporting here holds only more or less for the nine ditches of the valley and more certainly for the two ditches I irrigate from, the Jara and the Juntas. There are conceivably a thousand slightly different ways of apportioning water among the *parciantes* of each of the thousand *acequias* of New Mexico.

In theory, it probably makes sense to start a schedule at the top end of the ditch and work down, thereby saving the two or three hours it might take to fill the ditch up from one end to the other before starting, unless it proves necessary to favor neglected *parciantes* at the far end of the ditch or to vary the schedule for the sake of those whose times always fall after dark, particularly if the ditch remains on hours week after week. For a ditch with a hundred *parciantes* the paperwork can be considerable for every new weekly schedule, and a disruption can be exasperating for all concerned: the hours must then be recalculated, new *papelitos* written up and redistributed. Until a few years ago there were *parciantes* whose shares were only one-quarter *pión* each on the Acequia de las Juntas, the largest ditch in the valley with eighty-some *parciantes* in all, which at the worst meant that they were entitled to a quarter of an hour of water per week. Some of these small plots were also some distance below the ditch and were fed by lateral or feeder ditches—sometimes called *sangrias*—of up to a hundred yards long, and often the quarter-hour was used up just getting the water down to the distant gardens. After our last dry year, 1980, the ditch revised its regulations and made the smallest permissible share one-half *pión*.

Depending on which way the schedule is moving, there will be times when there is often unscheduled water available to whoever can get it. In the case of a downward-moving schedule, and in order to catch any water the upriver *parciantes* might happen to let go by, the alert *parciante* will leave his headgate open until the end of the hours for his place; and conversely, the schedule moving up the ditch, the *parciante* will keep his headgate closed until his hours begin and then leave it open after his hours are over.

In all this, as in all matters pertaining to ditches, the uppermost *parciantes* are in the most favorable position, the lowermost the least. Likewise for ditches in relation to each other as they take water from the river, whether their dams are above or below in the lineup. Size also has some bearing. A long ditch with many *parciantes* will have to go on hours much sooner than a small ditch with few *parciantes,* all things being equal; and the day of rationing can be put off when neighbors are in a mood to share what water there is, and hastened and aggravated by family or religious or racial feuding or mutual suspicion. And when hours begin, all kinds of things can go wrong. There will often be the *parciante* who decides to take water out of turn, plus the *parciante* who sleeps through his three A.M. schedule and misses his turn, or the one who misreads the hours on the *papelito,* and then there will be the unexpected problem at the *desagüe* that dries up the ditch right in the middle of the schedule, forcing the commission to improvise a new one for the remaining hours. Several years ago my wife and I were trying to irrigate the one-acre lower field at the Thompsons' within our allotted hours late one August afternoon when we were faced with two bewildering problems: a thunderstorm began sweeping in noisily from the west, and the ditch began to run dry. I left my wife working the water down the rows of corn with a hoe, while I set off with a shovel to walk the ditch in search of the dwindling water— until both our labors were halted by a thunderous, flashing downpour that soon ended the rationing for the week.

The Acequia de la Jara, with relatively few *parciantes* and perhaps more harmonious than many ditches, rarely has to go on hours, but for another reason. When the water starts running very low in the river, the level no longer holds steady: it gets lower and lower, faster and faster, as each of the ditches above us tightens up its dam, the whole sequence often triggered by the ditches in the valley ten miles above doing the same in response to a prolonged dry spell, usually in August. Often we don't have time to go on hours. When the river begins to run dry, we seal up our dam but the river continues to drop, and within a day or two there isn't enough water to reach the far end of the ditch.

When this used to happen we had no choice but to call for the dividing up of the river, often to the annoyance of those ditches above us that had just set up an elaborate schedule for their *parciantes*. They would always ask why we didn't go on hours ourselves. We would always respond that we didn't have enough water to go on hours with. And for us to try to convince the commissions and *mayordomos* of the six ditches whose dams lie within three-quarters of a mile of each other above ours to let a little more water go by for us down below became an impossible task in view of the chorus of several hundred *parciantes* all over the valley clamoring for more water. What also must not be forgotten is that each of those eighteen commissioners and six *mayordomos* had themselves a chile patch, an alfalfa field, an apple orchard which they considered in desperate need of water, not to speak of the little gardens of their aging parents and in-laws, *los viejitos,* on this or that other ditch. There were times when as commissioner of the Acequia de la Jara I had to stand by the pitiful little flow the river had become and argue with a commissioner from the Acequia de las Juntas over how much water he was going to let pass on to our dam a quarter of a mile below—both of us wondering how much would survive the passage across that barren desert of a river course—and then, agreement reached, immediately race over to the house of the Juntas *mayordomo* to find out when my hours on that ditch (where we own a two-acre field) were going to begin, changing hats, or faces, from that of impatient commissioner of one ditch to suppliant *parciante* of another during the hasty drive.

When things reach this state, as they last did in 1980, the *mayordomo* is often the first to crack. The *mayordomo* of the Acequia de las Juntas was then Joe Pacheco, a retired miner whose marginal literacy had until then not interfered with the running of the ditch, which he did well and fairly. But the distribution of nearly eighty *papelitos* to householders up and down the three-mile ditch for the weekly schedules turned out to be more than he could handle. One evening he and our *mayordomo* at the time, Paco Ortiz, drove up into the mountains and had a few drinks—no doubt to escape the endless stream of callers-in asking for water on both sides of the river. By the end of the evening Joe Pacheco was in jail, charged with a hit-and-run incident involving a kid on a bicycle, and over the next week the Juntas commission, besides having to administer to a confused and angry membership in a time of drought, found themselves strapped with the added burden of getting the poor man out of jail so he could continue on the job, and later guide him through two court hearings. A village wag suggested that our *mayordomo* got Joe Pacheco drunk in order to obtain somehow more water for our ditch. Not long after, Paco Ortiz tried to resign after a dispute with his nephew, but I managed to talk him into staying on.

The custom of dividing up the river may be of some antiquity or of relatively recent innovation; nobody seems to know. It has existed from a time well before I became a commissioner in 1970. I have heard it said that the ground rules were laid down years ago by the Office of the State Engineer in order to settle a dispute, but others have said there is no record of such an agreement in the agency files. Very possibly, a representative came out from Santa Fe and met with the ditches and without taking any formal action nonetheless suggested how the river might be equitably divided. Equally possible is that an agreement or a series of agreements have been in force for the past two hundred years but have been periodically forgotten, particularly in high-water years, or patchily remembered or revised, their memory carried fitfully forward from generation to generation by word of mouth until our recent current agreement was finally written down during the conference of local commissioners held in the winter of 1981.

The current river-sharing agreement among the eight ditches taking water from the upper one-mile stretch of the river sets the hour and the day of the week when the lower three ditches can take all the water, eight Sunday morning, as well as when the upper four ditches can take it back, eight Thursday morning each week. A lower ditch, the Acequia del Pueblo, is a nonparticipating signatory to the agreement; in recent memory the river has restored itself enough with springs below our dam to keep the Pueblo in water. During the four days down, the upper ditches (in theory) must close their headgates and let all the water pass; during the three days up, the lower ditches will be more or less without water. The reasoning behind the unequal division of days may lie in the fact that the lower ditches irrigate more land among themselves, and perhaps also to make up for the fact that the upper ditches begin to suffer much later from the effects of drought than the lower. When the lower ditches should *pedir el agua,* ask for the water, has long been a bone of contention and perhaps always will be, and those of us on the Acequia de la Jara, the lowermost and therefore first ditch to dry up, have most often been first to call for the dividing of the river.

Because of an abundance of water throughout most of the irrigating seasons since the summer of 1980, the terms of the agreement have not been exercised since then. Customarily, a delegation of lower-ditch commissioners would meet Sunday morning at a quarter to eight at the turnoff to Vallecito, usually two of us from the Acequia de la Jara, one or two from las Juntas, and one commissioner from los Cerritos. The five or six of us would then pile into one or two cars and drive up into Vallecito to collect padlock keys and combination lock numbers from the various *mayor-domos* and commissioners of the four upper ditches, a short drive of a mile or so during which we would discuss who was going to talk to whom and who we expected to have problems with on that particular morning, and how the previous week's irrigation schedules had gone with all our ditches. The county road along the south side of the valley climbs up above the sloping alfalfa fields and orchards and runs roller-coaster-fashion in and out of arroyos along the edge of piñon- and juniper-dotted hills that enclose the valley. Tin-roof adobes and mobile homes lie to the left, below the roadway, or perch on shelves carved out of the rocky hillsides or are tucked away in the mouths of arroyos to the right. The commuters to jobs in Los Alamos or the schools and hospitals own the larger houses where newer cars are parked, and

the odd-job and welfare families live in the houses
and trailers with yards often crowded with older cars
and trucks and junkers being scavenged for parts. In
the dry years of the late 1970s, four of us regularly
participated in what we jokingly called the Sunday
Morning Walking Society: Alberto Manzanares, commissioner from Los Cerritos, a stockily built man
whose at times ferocious appearance conceals a fine
sense of humor; Jimmy Ortiz, a wise and patiently
slow-speaking man with an excellent memory for the
intertwining genealogies of the valley and the histories of most local feuds among the Hispanic population, who accompanied a fellow commissioner from
the Acequia de las Juntas; John Polk, a writer of a
mystical bent who tutored me in the esoteric ways
of ditches and who had settled in the valley in the
mid-1960s, several years before a modest influx of
hippies and escapees from mainstream America had
begun subtly to alter the character of the area; and
then myself, the youngest and most inexperienced of
the group, and who was charged with representing
the smallest and "easiest" ditch in the valley, and
whose claim to be heard was that a few of us over
there in La Jara still more or less made a living off the
land. At various times other commissioners were part
of the delegation but in later years were either not reelected to their commissions or else "retired" after fifteen or twenty years of service; also, in my time, three

or four respected elders, all of them from the Acequia de las Juntas, have passed away.

Our first stop was usually the house of Pete López, commissioner of the small Acequia de los Pachecos which served no more than a dozen places across the river. López, a severe-looking man in his fifties with a round face and a sharp, nasal voice, was always good-natured and generous about dividing up the river. Year after year he gave us the combination to the head-gate lock with the words: "Do whatever you have to." In fact, he often urged us to ask for the water earlier.

A half-mile beyond his place the pavement runs out. The left fork of the now dirt road leads back down an arroyo to the river, where the narrowing track swings sharply right and runs along the river, separated from the boulder-strewn channel, deep and narrow through here, by a border of large cotton-woods. Opposite the right turn there is a narrow plank bridge under the private ownership of Cipriano López, the valley's most successful apple grower. The orchards run by Cipriano and his son Richard lie on a narrow strip of land immediately north of the river, perhaps ten or fifteen acres in all, and are served by a ditch whose status as a community association or private ditch has perhaps never been established. For years most of us down below have referred to it as "Cipriano's Ditch," not knowing whether in fact it has another name. It serves at most a half-dozen places. Cipriano López originally comes from southern Colorado and over the years has turned what must have seemed an unpromising patch of land into a model apple orchard that has yielded a crop almost without fail for decades, through the use of windmills, propane heaters, and the fortunate characteristics of the site. The winter cold hangs on later than in sunnier locations lower in the valley, holding back blossoming until the last minute, and of course the location of his ditch guarantees him an abundance of water. The feeling López always managed to convey to us, without ever being put into words, was that we didn't have the right to take any water from his ditch: the water was bestowed on us as a matter of courtesy, out of neighborliness. López never came to the meetings at which the written agreement was both worked out and then renewed two years later, though I believe he was given a copy of it. A dark man with an aristocratic manner, cigarette forever in hand, he would consent, through half-closed eyes and with a barely audible and almost whining drawl, to us taking "a little water" on our Sunday morning visits.

Back across Cipriano's bridge, then upriver, then back across another narrow bridge of wooden planks laid on steel beams, the road a narrow track now, we would drive past a couple of shacklike adobes, up onto a knoll where the track ended in the driveway to the last house on the north side of the river, a site that surveys the point where the valley narrows into a sloping funnel of lush grass and boulders and where the river emerges as a noisy torrent spilling out of a narrow box canyon a quarter of a mile to the east, below cliffs of dark basalt. This is another world up here, a world where nobody ever has water problems—until we arrive with our own. A short walk past the pitched-roof adobe brought us to the *desagüe* of Cipriano's Ditch where we would pry out a splashboard with a shovel and send most of the water swirling back down the grassy hillside to the river a hundred yards below. Usually we didn't completely cut off the flow to the ditch, and often left quite a lot of what had come to be called "water for the chickens"—a phrase that covered numerous nonirrigation uses of ditch water, including livestock and household uses for those few places still without running water at the time. Elaborate theories, transparently self-serving, were also concocted by some upper-ditch commissioners about how important it was to keep the channels of the upper ditches damp during the four days down. And how much chicken water we left was more a measure of how much we stood in fear of this or that upper-ditch commissioner, in the power of just one person to sabotage the whole agreement, than of need, which is why Cipriano López, the most prosperous farmer in the valley, always got more chicken water than all the other ditches serving over a hundred *parciantes* combined. The chickens in question were probably us.

On the opposite side of the river, south, the Acequia Rellena's head gate used to be presided over by a tough-talking fellow in his thirties, one Sam Giulio, half-Hispanic, half-Italian, who was an expert in raising objections to entering his property or taking any water from his ditch. Until recently he served as either *mayordomo* or as a commissioner on the Acequia Rellena. Its *desagüe* lies on his property, back of his house. It took me several years to see that he enjoyed the bluffing and the ceremoniousness of exchanging insults and threats, and that usually we could get whatever we wanted if only we would spend enough time convincing him of the necessity of our being there at eight every Sunday morning. Much of the talk in the car on the way up was often devoted to who was to take the lead in approaching Sam Giulio. Usually, Alberto Manzanares found himself chosen for the task: an equally skilled debater, he could be outspoken and even gruff when the occasion demanded, yet also knew how to retreat from an extreme or untenable position with humor and grace. In later years I usually told myself to keep quiet during the negotiations unless I felt that too much was being conceded; I tended to become too easily angry and impatient, and it took me a long time to understand the simple lesson that negotiations are best conducted dispassionately, no matter how much is at stake.

Giulio's place, the last on the south side of the river, lies up a cottonwood-bordered driveway which is a continuation of the road after it veers left to cross the plank bridge. It is very grassy and almost alpine through here in the summer, from the abundance of water sluiced over pastures from the ditch and also a spring that comes down an arroyo. There is often a mountain crispness to the morning air, even in August. Giulio would usually come out of his adobe house at the barking of his dogs and the slamming of car doors in his circular driveway, and then we would make our way together on foot up along the high ground of sodden pastures where his milk-cows wandered, and proceed up past a pigpen and chicken house and two or three old cars and trucks awaiting repairs. Following Sunday morning pleasantries about the weather or the fruit crop in his orchard, a dialogue would begin somewhat in this fashion:

"Okay, Giulio," Manzanares would say, the time having come to get down to business. His hearty tone could be heard as either challenging or slightly self-mocking. That would depend. "We've come to take all your water. We're not going to leave you a single drop."

Giulio would respond incredulously in his foghorn voice loud enough for even the hard of hearing: "Water? Come off it. You guys got plenty of water down there. All you gotta do is plug up your *regaderas* and all your leaks down there and you got plenty of water. You don't need any water from us. You've got more than you can use down there."

157

The argument would continue in this vein as we made our way slowly through the pasture uphill toward the gate. "I'll give you a little to help you guys out," Giulio would reluctantly concede. "But just a little. We just put a new schedule on for the ditch and we're going to have a bunch of angry *parciantes* if they don't get their water." The Acequia Rellena branches off from the river a quarter of a mile above Giulio's house and runs along the base of a cliff down to the *desagüe,* a concrete construction with a heavy gate which controls the water into the ditch via a siphon. A steel grate covers the mouth of the siphon under an arroyo perhaps thirty feet wide and which also marks the eastern end of the Giulio pasture. We would often stand at this structure and review the fine points of the annual debate while waiting for the exact hour to arrive. Giulio was never about to give us any water a minute before eight A.M. "You know what this is going to do to our *parciantes*," he would continue. "We're on hours. Why aren't you guys on hours down there?"

"How can we be on hours? We don't have any water."

"Ah, come on. I've seen the water at the bridge, there's plenty of water."

"At the bridge? Sure. That part of the river is fed by springs. Quarter of a mile up and the river is dry as a bone."

"You don't say."

The two-foot-diameter cast-iron wheel is secured

with a chain and a huge padlock. Over the years we were rarely entrusted with the key and often had to wait for the arrival of a late-sleeping *mayordomo* to come and unlock it—and face more arguments, even though *mayordomos* were not supposed to be involved in these negotiations. Giulio always managed to transcend such distinctions with his forceful presence: *mayordomo* or commissioner, he was still Sam Giulio. Padlock unfastened, we would then reach the dramatic point where the steel wheel must be turned to raise the guillotinelike gate, to flush the water back to the river and downstream toward our dams.

"Just two turns, that's enough."

We would protest. More turns would be conceded. We would stare down into the cement chamber to watch the water find its new level. One of the arguments against leaving any water for the chickens was that should the river rise, then much of the additional water would flow into the upper ditches instead of moving on down to the lower during our portion of the schedule. Often in the past we had to come back in the evening and insist on resetting the gates because the chicken water had become a major flow through such a change in the river.

Our dealings with Giulio usually concluded with his mock threats to walk up here and give the headgate wheel a few turns to his advantage later in the day. But over the years a sense of trust emerged from these contentious gatherings: we were all more or less predictable characters, and somewhere, at some level at least, we had the interests of the whole community at heart.

A quarter of a mile below Giulio's place the river channel widens out into bright ribbons of white sand dotted with bushel-basket-sized rocks. At this point the river is spanned by a seventy-five-foot concrete weir some five feet high which serves to direct water to two headgates at either end of it, that of the Acequia de los Pachecos to the north and the Acequia Central to the south. To reach the weir, we had to drive down a narrow sand track past the tangled wreckage of an old green Chevy pickup which was washed down an arroyo years ago—having been improvidently parked in the path of a flash flood—and through a copse of cottonwoods to a patch of solid ground where there is enough room to turn a car or truck around without getting stuck in the sand. From there we would walk the last hundred yards across a glaring expanse of sand and rocks patrolled by a pair of killdeer, usually arriving at the headgates ten minutes or so before the water we had just released from the ditches above. During a dry spell in summer the "river" is something you can step across from stone to stone without getting your feet wet. The added water never arrived with any noticeable flourish: we would stare at the bright sparkling pools in search of a slight murkiness, a few dead leaves floating down, a few more bubbles, signs that the additional water had caught up with us.

One or two of us would then hop across the fifty-foot expanse of rocks to the Acequia de los Pachecos head-gate, climb up on the cement wall and sit down straddling it and open the combination lock. The Pachecos was always the easiest: such is the justice of things that we never left its generous and fair-minded commissioner, Pete López, any water at all for the chickens. We would turn the big iron wheel and raise his gate high, throwing all the water back into the river, and then quickly hop back across the stones, but this time getting our feet wet.

The Acequia Central to the south was another matter. The second largest ditch in the valley, it was also perhaps the second-most contentious. Usually, they would let us regulate the water without one of their commissioners being present as long as we were careful to leave quite a lot of chicken water. Years ago, long and drawn-out disputes with their *mayordomo* over regulating their headgate led to the commissioners of the lower ditches refusing to deal with him, insisting on what was believed to be an old rule to the effect that *mayordomos* were to take care of internal affairs and leave foreign relations to the commissions.

After setting the Acequia Central headgate to let a small flow of chicken water down their ditch, the river was now ours, or mostly ours, for the next four days. By nine or nine-thirty on Sunday morning, all going well, we would finish turning off the headgates of the four upper ditches and the water would be heading on down the arid channel toward the dams of the Acequia de los Cerritos first, then, the Acequia de las Juntas, and lastly to ours, the Acequia de la Jara, a half-mile run through rocks and boulders bleached white in the sun, a channel that became increasingly drier and more desertlike as it approached our dam. In the worst of years the river was completely dry those last two hundred yards except for the occasional pool of still, greenish water in the shade of an over-hanging cottonwood tree. Probably a third, perhaps even half the water we took from the upper ditches simply disappeared into the sand on its way down-river, and it was often difficult to judge how much water would be available at the dams below. If the flow was good and the drought not far advanced, then we could all count on going home and waiting for the water to come down our ditches, in the hope that our respective *mayordomos* could deal with it from then on. This supposed, of course, that the water would automatically divide itself equitably between our three lower dams.

Sometimes it did, but more often it didn't, and the Sunday morning drive back down through Vallecitos to the turnoff would usually be consumed in deciding whether to meet again at ten-thirty at the Cerritos dam or to wait until later in the morning to see how much water was coming down our ditches. Naturally, as the representative of the lowermost of the ditches, I was most anxious not to disband the group until we were certain what we would be obtaining our share of the water. I always maintained that it would be better to follow the water through the two higher dams then and there and be done with it, but often I compromised and agreed to telephone the Juntas and Cerritos commissioners by a certain hour, usually noon, if I was unsatisifed with what we were getting, exacting promises that everyone would stay within reach of their phones until then. On rare occasions dividing up the river could be done by nine Sunday morning, and the water would reach the far end of our ditch, the property of our next to the last and most desperate *parciante,* Reynaldo Vasques, by two Sunday afternoon. Far more often noon or one o'clock would roll around and we would find only a small flow in the upper part of our ditch. Soon the lower *parciantes* would be driving around and asking when water would be getting to their places. In the absence of a schedule everyone is anxious to water first in case something happens, as indeed it often does.

As a commissioner in those days I was usually the first one to get on the phone and announce the bad news that the Cerritos and Junta ditches were not letting enough water past their dams for us and that we had all better meet again, this time at Alberto Manzanares's place in Los Cerritos. A corner of his property was next to our dam, a walk across a pasture from his house, if the other commissioners wanted to have a look at how little water we were receiving from above. But usually we would just climb back into Alberto's car and drive straight up to an orchard owned by Pete López further up in Los Cerritos, where we would park and walk down through the apple trees to a narrow stretch of the river blocked off by the rock-and-brush construction that made up the Cerritos dam. Alberto, a chemist who has spent much of his working life at the Plutonium Facility in Los Alamos, was the one who came to call us the Sunday Morning Walking Society on one of our numerous hikes, and in time I came to trust and respect him for his fairness in the difficult negotiations. His own place, an apple orchard and large pasture that produced a good stand of thick grass in the damp bottomland of Los Cerritos, was happily served by two ditches, the Acequia de los Pachecos and the Acequia de los Cerritos, the first an upper, the second a lower, which meant that he was rarely without water, no doubt an aid to even-handedness. Whenever possible I brought along one of my fellow commissioners, either to back me up or to train for future water-sharing sessions when I might not be able to be there. In the early 1970s, Jerry Munster and I often went for water together. Later, in the dry years at the end of the decade, Larry Bustos and Arthur Litton became frequent participants in the Sunday Morning Walking Society.

Upon moving a few rocks—and sometimes the discussion would center on *which* rock we could move—and removing usually a splashboard in the

Cerritos *desagüe,* we would then hike back to the car and drive all the way down through Los Cerritos to the highway, cross the river, and drive a half-mile back up into Vallecitos and turn off down into a narrow, twisting arroyo, and follow a sandy track down to a low bluff below which ran the Acequia de las Juntas. The Juntas had two *desagües* along here and rather than rearrange the rocks or splashboards at their concrete weir of a dam, they preferred that we take water from one of the *desagües.* At this point the terms and participants shifted, like musical chairs. At the Cerritos dam, the line was often drawn between four Jara and Juntas commissioners and Alberto Manzanares alone, though he was quite capable of defending the interests of his ditch against our bullying. Now, at the Juntas *desagüe,* he joined La Jara to help us argue the needs of our thirty *parciantes* against the eighty or so of Las Juntas—in a situation where I had interests on both sides of the dispute. And by now it was usually hot, the day was fleeing, and all of us were worried about whether we would have enough water to irrigate our own individual places. With luck, on those Sundays we followed the water all the way down, occasionally walking the whole distance between the Cerritos and Jara dams, we could disband the Sunday Morning Walking Society by twelve-thirty or one, after four or five hours of driving, haggling, walking.

During the worst years we had to go bring the

water down four or five Sundays in a row, and one autumn we were at it for seven weeks running. Gradually I learned to insist on a generous share of water for La Jara during the initial settings, with the argument that this would spare us the necessity of reconvening the group later in the day. Before, less cunning, we frequently found ourselves in the situation of having to gather the other ditch commissioners together again Sunday afternoon or evening, take them to our dam, show them how little water was coming down to us, go through the readjustments yet one more time. Driving around the valley and walking up and down the river and through apple orchards in the heat of an August afternoon was not something any of us much wanted to do, and often, by midafternoon, apathy would become the final arbiter of how much water each ditch obtained from the modest flow. Blatant inequities, of course, could always be turned into scoring points the following week.

As *mayordomo* I am not a participant in the Sunday Morning Walking Society, which in fact has not been active since 1981, although under the agreement we have twice asked for water since then, only to have the rains arrive before the appointed day for dividing the river. In a dry year the work of bringing down the water and then rationing it to the *parciantes* of each ditch can become a full-time job in itself, to the point that commissioners and *mayordomos* can know a strange sense of relief when, on Thursday mornings, the water passes back up to the upper ditches. When the ditch is dry for those three days you can at least think of something else besides water. And though water negotiations can be tedious and contentious, when a drought reaches a certain point a sense of community can arise out of the emergency and push aside many of the old differences, breaking up the terms of the ritualistic debates. Our worst time was the summer of 1981, when the water level in the river dropped so precipitously in August that the commissioners of all nine ditches held two meetings within days of each other, so fast was it becoming apparent that there was not enough water to divide among even three or four ditches at a time. The river was no longer lowering, it was beginning to disappear altogether. The first crisis was precipitated by the upper ditches when they began fighting among themselves during their three-day portion of the schedule; they called upon the lower ditches to help them set up a new arrangement. The first meeting was held on Harold Castillo's lawn, on a terrace gouged out of the hillside above Los Cerritos, on a hot, clear evening, with swallows, swifts, nighthawks, and bats carving up the darkening sky of a panorama that extended from the mountains to the east almost the whole length of the valley to the west, reminding us that we all lived in one place and drew water from one source. In this gracious, almost Mediterranean setting, we worked out a provisional arrangement that further sudivided our system of three days up and four days down, but the weather stayed searingly hot and dry and the river continued to evaporate, and we were back meeting in the school yard several nights later in the gathering darkness of thunderheads rising to the west. Shadows to each other, we perched on the school yard merry-go-rounds, slides, teeter-totters, sandboxes, now and then illuminated by flashes of lightning. The sky rumbled and growled as we argued with each other into the night and heard accusations of cheating and hogging, and waited for the peacemakers to come forth and urge patience and understanding and to remind us again of the one community of which we all formed part, whatever our many differences. Thirty people were there. With difficulty, we all finally agreed that each ditch would take the whole river for roughly one day of the week. The largest two ditches would have slightly more than twenty-four hours each, the smaller five slightly less than that, while the eighth and ninth ditches would continue to be served by the springs that were still reviving the river several hundred yards below the desert where our dam stood. And during the coming week all ditches would close their headgates completely in order to allow all the water in the river to flow into the ditch whose turn it was each day. There would be no more water for the chickens anywhere. Perhaps that night we all realized that the lower the water in the river, the drier the season, the more people come to be involved in distributing the water throughout the valley, and that when it gets as bad as this then virtually everyone in the village becomes intimately involved: from then on, every time someone opened or closed a ditch gate on their land, a thousand people would be watching and listening.

Later that night it began to rain. Then to pour—as if the skies were saying that as soon as we all managed to cooperate among ourselves, then one way or the other there would be enough water for everyone.

Eight

During times of plentiful water a *parciante* can often take whatever he can use from a ditch, regardless of how many *piones* or shares his place is: the value of a *pión* as a share comes alive only when water becomes scarce. There are always limits, of course, to how much water most *parciantes* can use, through the size of feeder ditches, for example, or the generally detrimental effects of constantly flooding a field. During times of rationing the *pión* assumes a strict value in the form of a certain number of hours per week a *parciante* has the right to take water from the ditch, rationing which may be either a matter of regular practice in a ditch with numerous *parciantes* and a limited source of water, or an exceptional measure brought on by drought. In much the same way that a share of stock is ideally related to the worth and productivity of a corporation, as also a function of complex market and financial factors, so the value of the *pión* as an amount of available water will be a function of a mountain snowpack, summer rains, the competence of a commission and *mayordomo,* the character of fellow *parciantes,* in addition to the location of the property holding the *pión* in relation to other water users—not to speak of the competence of all those other commissioners whose ditches will be taking water from the same stretch of river. At the one extreme, the value of a *pión* will be linked to the position of the jet stream, which will determine in part how wet or dry a season will be, or to how many volcanoes have recently spewed particulate matter into the upper atmosphere, and at the other extreme, the habits of beavers, muskrats, gophers, crayfish, whose workings can disable a ditch during the best of seasons. If all goes well, a *pión* of water will on some ditches be almost limitless. By the same token a flood or a feud within a ditch or among ditches competing for the same water can render a *pión* worthless for various periods of time.

As a share, as a proportion of a varying whole, in traditional situations the *pión* is nowhere firmly tied to a fixed unit of measure. No *pión* on one ditch will be "worth" the same on any other ditch, no more than the share of one corporation will be worth that of any other, except coincidentally. *Piones* are generally thought to be tied to acreage, and in a vague sense they are. But the acre as a unit of measure has come into use in northern New Mexico only recently, with the advent of surveying practices in which both square footage and boundaries are important for mortgaging purposes. Traditional land transfers among Hispanic families concerned themselves mainly with boundary points and lines and paid much less attention to acres or other units of square measure, and I have never heard a *pión* described in terms of a quantity of water needed to irrigate a specific area of land: a *pión* refers to a share of water available from an *acequia,* not to any fixed area of land to be irrigated. By implication, in a traditional situation, a farmer will vary the size of his plantings and the nature of his cropping practices to accord with his expectations of how much water his *pión* will be worth during any particular irrigation season. This seems commonsensical enough, and if I labor the point it is because the adjudication of water rights tends in its effects to devalue traditional percep-tions and practices in favor of more abstract and mar-ket-oriented quantifications.

Piones, unlike shares of stock, are not transferable outside the *parciantes* of a ditch. A commission can raise or lower the number of *piones* per property, in theory at least, though this is not codified in any way, and most ditches whose workings I have knowledge of are uncertain of their powers here. The *pión* is a share of water in the ditch: it is not, however, a water right in relation to a river, which is granted by the state. Under Spanish water law, water and land go together, and are not transferred or sold separately from one another. In theory a *parciante* can lose the right to take water from a ditch by failing to use it for a certain number or years or by failing to pay fees or supply labor required of all *parciantes,* but he has no firm legal and therefore financial grounds to dispose of his water rights separately from his land. Further, ditches do not own water, they only transport it: a ditch commission controls not water rights but, in effect, delivery rights. Spanish water law was set into place in a time before deep wells, massive diversion and storage dams, and before the flows of streams and rivers could be accurately measured, and of course before the various intrastate and regional and international water compacts were created in the southwestern United States. In the face of these developments, traditional water-use arrangements, which still hold over unadjudicated portions of stream systems in New Mexico, appear conservative and even reactionary, an obstacle to economic progress and development. So in fact they are.

Through adjudication of water rights a share of a variable amount of water entering an *acequia's* headgate is, in effect, replaced by a fixed share measured in acre feet of a much larger and less variable whole that consists of an entire regional stream system; a certain rigidity is created at the local level in the interests of quantification and flexibility at the regional level. The traditional arrangement is myopic: it looks at a short stretch of river and whatever water happens to be there at the time it divides up among the *acequias* and, within the *acequias,* among *parciantes,* and each *parciante*'s share, his *pión,* varies roughly according to how much water is in the river at that particular point and time. Adjudication and the various regulatory steps that precede or follow it also create a new hierarchy of water users, replacing an oral tradition, in which uses are constantly under negotiation, with one based on a system of documentary evidence.

Each way no doubt has its virtues; sometimes, no doubt, the effects of adjudication and the establishment of water rights and priority dates for irrigation are equitable and fair, and no doubt often they are not. But the main effect of adjudication is that once the process is completed, then a water right becomes a commodity that can be rented or leased or sold anywhere within the state of New Mexico, subject to the approval of the Office of the State Engineer. Upon adjudication, a water right enters a vastly larger market that has nothing to do with the land it was once attached to, or with *acequias,* their commissions, or the community of which it once formed part. This might not be objectionable if the sale of a water right were not, in effect, also the sale, or rather dispersal, of part of an *acequia,* a part of a community at the same time. Without water rights a *parciante* ceases to be one, and a ditch loses thus a member, a taxpayer, a *pión,* a potential worker, a potential officeholder. The

pión is each *parciante*'s share in a corporation that consists of his community, giving him a vote in the conduct of his community's affairs, qualifying him for
office within his community, offering him a measure
of easily accessible public responsibility that may be
becoming increasingly unusual in public life in the
United States.

With its interminable court hearings, the adjudicat-
ing process can sweep through a community and un-
dermine traditional arrangements that have stood in
place for hundreds of years, in order to convert what
has been held in common to that which can be owned
privately. The bias and intention of water-rights adjudication is obvious: to serve the regional water market and facilitate the transfer of water rights from
rural, water-rich but economically dormant areas to
the expanding metropolitan areas of the arid south. If
northern New Mexico succumbs to the pressure to
convert water from the uses of subsistence agriculture
to municipal-industrial uses for the cities of Santa Fe,
Albuquerque, and Las Cruces, something irreplace-
able of a political and cultural nature will be seriously
endangered. There are few other civic institutions left
in this country in which members have as much control over an important aspect of their lives; relatively
autonomous, in theory democratic, the thousand *acequias* of New Mexico form a cultural web of almost
microscopic strands and filaments that have held a
culture and a landscape in place for hundreds of years.

What is remarkable is how well the *acequia* tradition has been kept alive deep within a larger Hispanic colonial tradition of government that has often favored absolutism over more participatory arrangements. And as the costly and socially disruptive process of adjudication is carried out throughout the north, often pitting traditional Pueblo and Hispanic communities against each other, one may fairly ask whether it is more important for water to feed material values than social or civic ones. Perhaps our logic has got turned upside down: in the north we should be saying that water is essential for keeping our communities together, and such is its main use now—as the substance around which a most remarkable tradition of self-governance adheres. To this, even agricultural use may be secondary.

The three-mile stretch of the Rio de la Junta, as I have called it, which runs through our valley and from which nine *acequias* feed, has not yet been adjudicated. We have that to look forward to in the future. As a small community we will probably not undergo the prolonged agony of the *State Engineer vs. Aamodt et al.,* a suit that will adjudicate the waters claimed by the Pueblos of Nambé, Pojoaque, and San Ildefonso, and the mixed Hispanic-Anglo communities of Nambé and Pojoaque, and which has dragged on for nearly twenty years now and at a cost of over three million dollars, and which has involved the U.S. Congress, the Bureau of Indian Affairs, tribal councils, local *acequias* and citizens' groups, and innumerable lawyers on all sides—and to who knows what ultimate social costs within these historically intertwined communities. But besides being most obviously a sad use of public and private funds, the Aamodt suit is also a measure of the resources state and federal agencies are willing to marshal at the service ultimately of urban economic development.

Nine

During the past several years the annual weather pattern has shifted to give us dry winters and summers and wet springs and autumns. This summer has proven to be a very dry one in the valley, yet enough rain has fallen in the mountains to keep all the ditches running without our having to resort to dividing the river. But right after Labor Day the weather turns unseasonably cold, running a month or more ahead of itself, the sky brightening to a clear and open blue when it should still be holding a protective mellow haze, and the sun seems to drop a few degrees closer to the horizon. On such days you feel the sky has opened up to the infinite coldness of outer space. Were this early October, not early September, I would turn on the weather radio and set the thermometers to register the first frost. But now, so early, I am only disheartened. Even if a frost is predicted I still have so much produce out in the field I wouldn't know where to begin: what I could gather up in the truck or throw covers over would be but a fraction of what I would lose in chile, winter squash, pumpkins.

I try to ignore the bright cold. And the ditch has to be kept running, no matter what. The modest salary covers me until the end of September. The water has gone down the last few days, and I finally rouse myself from my torpor and drive up to the dam in the faint warmth of an afternoon. The water runs in a bright clear sheet over the dying brown algae covering the rocks as it angles across the barren channel toward the funnel of our dam, not yet too cold to work in. I need to move a few rocks and plug some holes, and I spend a half hour in the diminished, quiet water, mourning the passing of another summer, wishing back the heat I was cursing only a month ago. On the river bottom, in the water six inches to a foot deep, I leave scars of grey where my shoveling and dragging have scraped algae off the stones and gravel. I manage to increase the flow slightly; unless it rains, I'll have to come back soon with a helper or two to lay a sheet of black plastic across the dam to seal up the cracks. No *parciantes* have called for water, but I can't believe there's enough to irrigate with at the far end of the ditch. Normally after about mid-September most people let their fields dry up, aside for a last irrigation for orchards and alfalfa fields if there is enough water.

I'm the only regular autumn planter with my garlic and Walla Walla sweet onions and, when I can find the time, winter rye as a green manure crop to be tilled under in spring. But it's still early in September: perhaps nobody has called because they are as bewildered by the weather as I am.

The cold front moves on without giving us a frost in the end, and through the first two weeks of September the ditch remains low. Toward midmonth we have two light rains in a row, enough to settle the dust and wash clean the still green but wearying leaves of cottonwoods and apple trees, the upreaching leaves of squash and gourd vines, pale and yellowing now in their disappointment in the diminishing sunlight that is reaching their cupped forms. Often this time of year we have a good arroyo-washing storm, fruit of moist air pushed westward to our mountains by Gulf Coast hurricanes, which recharges the watershed and fills up the river until winter, and whose lightning bolts precipitate a last foliar feeding of nitrogen for the plants, but this year we must settle for less. Creeper on fencelines begins here and there to turn red as a harbinger of frost, and the occasional apple, pear, plum floats down the ditch, beginnings of what will soon become a long procession of bright leaves, orange, red, gold, along with the bobbing fruit, through the clear days and crisp nights for weeks on end, toward the distant Gulf waters which feed our rains and snows. Water, which has given the earth life these past months, now begins its work of dissolution, liquefaction, decay, the washing away in bright sinuous strands to feed the far oceans: its labor, like ours, changes with the seasons.

The cool weather hangs on through the month. The first frost is likely to be hard: there will be no light topping frost as a first warning, to be followed a week or ten days later by the real thing, with that helpful interval in between in which to strip the fields of everything that can be stored or sold. By the end of the month I have heaped my pumpkins and covered them with cornstalks and have moved most of the winter squash out of the field to a pile on the west side of my shed where I can throw a tarp over them at night; I have readied plastic to go over the best part of the tomato row; the globe amaranth is pulled up and ready to be hung from the shed rafters; and whenever I have a moment I pick a few apples from the laden trees at the Thompson place. I mostly think of how much everything weighs. The water I have guided down the ditch all summer and along the rows of my fields has metamorphosed into squash, pumpkins, chile, apples, onions, which I must lift endlessly up off the ground and in and out of the truck, into the shed, back into the truck, out of the truck at market, bringing home what's left over, carrying it back into the shed: what was once so fluid now hardened into the bright protean spheres and pods, carted about in old wooden boxes.

Mayordomo

One day in late September I drive up to Los Cerritos and swing down the narrow track that becomes Nick Manzanares's driveway and roll down past a small garden where chile pods are turning bright red. I park at Nick's empty round adobe house. The color of tourmaline, the ditch runs darkly between its grassy banks at the edge of the lawn, a good chirping flow, better than I had been led to expect from the trickle passing by our house. The lower *desagüe* turns out to be blocked at the entrance with a dam of twigs and brush that looks easy to pull out: I am in luck, I won't have to drive up to the dam. On hands and knees I fish out the debris. The water is warm. The early fall has caught it by surprise: its warmth betrays it as a living thing.

On Wednesday, November 27, the day before Thanksgiving, on a mild and clear afternoon I drive up to the lower *desagüe* one last time to shut off the ditch for the winter. The water has continued running very low for a month or so, a leaf-clogged trickle that reaches my place but probably not to the very end. From October on nobody irrigates, though I continue to run a dribble for my geese as long as there is water, and other *parciantes* with livestock use the ditch in the same way. At the *desagüe* I pry out the splashboards with a shovel and send the water, such as it is, back to the river. Then I lower the wooden gate across the mouth of the ditch and shovel back into the channel the mound of sand on the bank, to build up a berm across it a few paces beyond the gate, just before the leaning cottonwood. By this time of year damp ground in shady places is usually frozen but we have finally had a wet autumn alternating with warm spells, one of which we are now in the middle of, and the ground has not yet frozen anywhere. The berm will probably freeze in a couple of weeks and thus become a secure barrier against water coming into the ditch beyond the *desagüe* until we are again ready for it late next March. A sheet of black plastic lines the stone dike just before the cement portion of the *desagüe;* when I pull it out and knock down the stones with my shovel, water coming from the dam will have two exits out of the *desagüe* back to the river. Beavers or wind-blown tumbleweeds or even inventive human beings can send water unexpectedly down a channel thought to be closed off, so the more ways out for it the better.

Curious to see what is going on at the dam and hoping that there might be a way I could shut off the water even up there, I drive on up. I have thought of calling out a small crew to close off the channel right below the dam, but have never got around to it. At the upper *desagüe* at the bottom of Harold Castillo's orchard, beavers again: more trees down, and the channel appears to be almost completely blocked a hundred yards down, somewhere near José Castillo's pasture, to judge from the slow-moving lagoon that

184

stretches out of sight down the ditch. I follow the bank down to investigate. Blackened leaves and twigs float in the deep still water of the four-foot-wide pond. The obstacle, a massive tangle of muddy branches and twigs at the fence dividing José's and Rupert's fields, proves to be unyielding to my half-hearted efforts. The afternoon is too chilly to get oneself wet in, and it occurs to me that it would be better to leave things as they are. The beaver's construction, its final triumph of the season, may do what I cannot: shut the water off between the two *desagües*. So for the winter I turn the ditch, or this hundred-yard segment of it, over to the beavers.

Yet as I walk back up the bank, I consider that the water ought to go somewhere. If the lagoon freezes solid, as could happen in January, it could cause the bank to heave. Back at the *desagüe* I set about clearing slimy twigs and branches out of two narrow channels so that water can drain back into the river at the culvert, slow pick-up-sticks work groping around in the cold water on hands and knees from the bank. A few of the larger branches I lay across the mouth of the culvert in the hope that the next logjam will take place there and thus perhaps send all of the water back into the river by the time spring comes.

After half an hour of this I am cold and wet enough to call it an afternoon, gather up my tools and gloves and hike back up through Harold's orchard to my truck parked up at the road. There is nothing more to do on the ditch until March, and until then I can forget about it all, forget about whether there's enough water or too much, about who's not getting enough, who's taking too much, about beavers and muskrats, and they at last can forget about me. Now winter can come. I am pleased even at the final clatter my rake and shovel make as I lower them into the bed of the pickup.

Yes, now everything can freeze.

Ten

I learned of the suicide of Ignacio Serna, one of our commissioners, the night my wife and two teenage children drove in from a two-week stay in California, Sunday, the fifth of January 1986. "The man in the first house," the friends who had been sitting our place told us. Coming back to a village where you know virtually everybody is often like this: the shock of learning who has died, who has fallen ill, the car wrecks, fires, marriages broken up. Poor Ignacio. I was certain it was him from our friends' description of the house. Next day at the post office and the store, I heard the details from those I ran into. I had known that Ignacio had not been working since midsummer when he was involved in a freak accident in the parking lot of the Los Alamos school, where he worked the night shift as a janitor. At around two in the morning while Ignacio was walking around the front of his car to get in and drive home, a drunken teenage driver ran into him and threw him against the front of the car; he suffered a concussion, a broken rib, and injuries to his legs that were to require skin grafts. He himself did not remember what happened: by helicopter he was flown unconscious to the University of New Mexico Trauma Center in Albuquerque, where he regained consciousness. After a week in the hospital he was sent home to recuperate. I visited him once at home in August when he was still bedridden, lying shirtless in a hospital bed in the living room next to the front door, legs covered, complaining and in pain yet able to summon a measure of good humor about his condition—and appearing, incongruously, in robust health. Because his sons were grown, I always thought of him as older than myself when, in fact, he was probably the same age or even younger, in his late forties. In the past Ignacio and I had always conducted our business out in his driveway. My bedside visit would have been perhaps the first time I had actually stepped inside the Serna house, and Mrs. Serna, a small, shy woman, hovered in the background, smiling in embarrassment or perhaps overwhelmed by the fact that the stranger had finally condescended to enter the door. By the end of the summer Ignacio was walking again and soon driving, though I heard he had not yet gone back to work; whenever I ran into him at the store or post office he seemed in good enough spirits. I never expected him to be an active commissioner, no more than for the ritual signing of my checks, so his incapacity had no effect on the operation of the ditch. But apparently the eventual effect of the concussion—or worse—was to send him into a deep depression for which he began to undergo some kind of therapy toward the end of the year. In December his therapist had even told him to stop driving.

A couple of days after returning from California, I drove up to the Serna house to pay my respects to the widow and sons. Mateo was there, and Mrs. Serna was sitting forlornly in the small dining room behind a table laden with casseroles and pies and cakes. The son invited me to sit down in the adjoining living room, equally small, in a chair next to where his father's hospital bed had once been placed, next to the front door. I was served some food—I no longer remember what. I asked Mateo what had happened, explaining I had been away during it all and though I had seen a few people since my return I still didn't have a clear sense of how or why his father had come to such a point of desperation. Over the next half hour, a time when his two brothers, one younger, one older, came and went, Mateo recounted the progress of his father's deepening depression and how he seemed somehow unable to recover from the accident despite the appearances of improving health. While the rest of them were sleeping, the morning of New Year's Day, Ignacio got up and took out his .30-caliber rifle from its place in a closet and stepped out into the backyard, a space demarked by the curving course of the barren ditch bank as it wends its way across the property toward the Thompson place: dry weeds, a few apple trees, the ramshackle chicken and pig pens built up against the ditch bank, piles of old scrap lumber probably coated with frost that morning, and the usual abandoned refrigerator, hot-water-heater tank. Beyond, to the north, through the apple trees, the simple two- or three-room adobe house of his ninety-year-old father, and then beyond that, the clay and gravel hills dotted with stunted piñons and junipers, and a sky whose morning flames of haze would have soon burned off to unveil the eggshell blue of winter sky. The sound of a solitary shot early in the morning would not of itself be considered unusual at sunrise in the neighborhood: many a pig has seen the last light in the almost ceremonious slaughter called *la matanza*. But this would have been louder than the usual .22. It woke the family. Mateo was the first outside. He found his father stretched out behind the house. "He was still trembling," he told me.

Ignacio Serna was buried a few days later in the small Baptist cemetery that populates a rocky slope of barren ground just above the entrance to Los Cerritos, a quarter of a mile above his house, amid simple wooden crosses, with fading plastic flowers atop mounds of sandy earth and rocks that suggest heaps of blankets piled atop the forms of sleepers, and with a view of a narrow section of the valley just upriver from where he lived, and of the immense sky that you become conscious of the moment you drive up out of the valley toward the mountains. The community was shocked by his death; his was, I was told, a huge funeral. Being honored with the title of commissioner of the Acequia de la Jara was finally not enough to save Ignacio Serna from the world, and finally from himself, from his demons, from the slight tug against cold metal, the sharp metallic taste in the mouth that would make it all go away. He joined his eldest son, victim of an accidental shooting some ten years before. Several days after the son's funeral, my wife and I, on an evening walk, came across Ignacio and his wife sitting in the dirt on the edge of the road opposite their house—as if they had set out on foot to try to escape their grief but had been struck down again by it just outside their gate and, overcome, had slumped to the ground. That is probably how I will always remember him.

Although the winter often seems long, the new irrigation season always comes sooner than expected in the form of small preparatory tasks. As *mayordomo,* I should inspect at least the dam and the upper part of the ditch before the annual meeting in March, and should also have put my work-crew records into order and handed them over to the commission to enter into the account book. The commission, in turn, should try to collect *delincuencias* over the winter so that we can start the new season with some money in the bank to pay for extra workers directly should our *parciantes* not send enough *piones*. And this year we must begin earlier than usual. Sandra Jackson has been working with the Soil Conservation Service on a plan to replace our two *desagües* with new ones. At the 1985 annual meeting we appointed her fiscal agent for the project, and since then she has been filling out forms for the one state and two federal agencies involved and has met with SCS agents and engineers and prospective contractors innumerable times, often tramping down through Harold Castillo's orchard with them to inspect the principal construction site, all this in the face of various filing deadlines and staff cutbacks all through the government. Gas company, electric co-op, highway department all had to be dealt with to secure releases of various kinds, and the *parciantes* kept informed of the progress and intricacies of the application procedure so they wouldn't end up feeling as if they were buying something they didn't really want or that someone might be personally benefiting from the project. Guiding it toward completion was, in effect, a sizable part-time job in itself, for which she received no compensation—other than, as ditch treasurer, the usual exemption from work-crew contributions or fees. I was delighted when she took interest in the prospective project at our annual meeting a year ago; she is a very determined woman, a good organizer, and I felt she was a match for the government agencies and their rivers of paperwork which had managed to discourage previous commissions from proceeding beyond the most preliminary steps.

Around noon on an unseasonably warm Sunday late in February, I drive up to see Harold Castillo, to ask his permission to run a couple of cement trucks down through his orchard for the building of the new *desagüe,* to begin in about a month, all going well. Harold's house sits up above the road to the north on a ledge carved out of the reddish clay and gravel of the hills ranging the north side of the valley, up a steep driveway. A two-story balconied garage-workshop is built back into the side of the hill, with a lawn separating it from a ranch-style cement-block house with an expanse of plate glass facing out over the valley. A moment after my honking, from a side patio door Harold emerges, dressed in grey slacks and a striped dress shirt, having probably stepped away from an after-church Sunday dinner. He is a boyish-looking man in his forties, with a strong pointed jaw and a shock of black hair lying flat across his head.

I apologize for disturbing him and then explain our request. I have asked Harold favors like this over the years and know that his first response is often tight-lipped and breath-holding, but I also know that if I continue to explain he will relent and even become friendly. I once offended him by ordering a couple of cottonwoods felled at the dam, the zeal of the moment overcoming my better judgment. They stood on the ditch bank and would, when felled, drop across the ditch and into the river, then running high, and thus form the beginnings of a dam. But we were no better in our aim than beavers: the two large cottonwoods, one after another, sailed merrily away in the brown flood as we watched helplessly from the rocky bank. Harold later maintained that we had endangered the river bank along his property and were depriving him of shade trees at a spot where he and his family like to sit at the end of the day in summer, next to the river. He was entirely right, and I later apologized. But since then, beavers working down there have taken down most of the rest of the big trees along his fenceline, and in the perspective of their work I think my own offense came in time to seem minor.

I explain that the Soil Conservation Service regards the river as too unstable along his land for us to build a permanent dam, which would of course help protect his field from being eroded away at the southwest corner, but at the prohibitive expense of channeling the river for a quarter of a mile upstream. But the SCS has approved funding for a *desagüe,* and the commission is about to open the job for bids. Harold's permission to enter his orchard property is crucial to build the works; the only other way in there would be up or down the river course, possible for bulldozers and backhoes but not for gravel and cement trucks. Doubtless any investment in ditch works would provide an incentive for the government to protect the river banks all along there or rebuild them after major floods: Harold would thus obtain some advantage from our relatively minor project.

He is reasonable, it turns out, and we settle on four or five points of a letter of agreement concerning replacing fences, compensating for damages, and so on. In the course of our conversation we walk across the lawn and step over to the edge of the terrace and look down. Years ago this is where the commissions of eight ditches met to decide how to carve up the river whose flow was shrinking rapidly each day. Thirty feet below lies the dirt road through Los Cerritos, then immediately below that the fence along the upper side of his orchard and the dry, weed-grown channel of the Acequia de los Cerritos, which passes through a steel culvert under the track into the orchard along the western fenceline, down a slope toward our ditch and the river a tenth of a mile to the south. I have walked that path countless times down past his pile of Los Alamos salvage over the past fifteen years or so without noticing that, in fact, it is quite wide enough for a cement truck to pass without snagging more than a couple of branches; only the culvert now seems a little narrow. We amble back to my pickup and I thank Harold for granting us access through his property. He replies that his ditch, the Cerritos, has a similar arrangement through Pete López's orchard, and his parting words, "We have to help each other out," though uttered somewhat severely are, I believe, entirely heartfelt.

On my way home I see Irwin, Mateo, and another who looks vaguely familiar standing in the yard of the Serna place, so I pull in. The third person turns out to be Jacob Pacheco, up from Albuquerque on vacation and much fleshed out from a skinny kid of a couple of years ago. Round face now even rounder, hooded eyes behind thick glasses, and that lightly accented, squeezed-out nasal voice as ever. Some years ago, not yet twenty, he served as a commissioner on our ditch for a season. At the time he was driving a black Pontiac Grand Prix hardtop, the premiere low-rider car in northern New Mexico, which he had lowered to within inches of the pavement. Arthur Litton and I were the other two commissioners at the time, and one afternoon we all went out collecting, *andando colectando,* in the long black car, complex symbol of young Hispanic pride and defiance, whose lowness precluded us from visiting those *parciantes* who had bumpy driveways. I sat in the front, Arthur in the back, as we crept along bouncily, and when some friends of mine drove past I remember turning to Jacob and saying, "I wonder what my friends are going to think when they see me riding around in a low-rider." He turned to me and shot back: "What are *my* friends going to say when they see me driving a bunch of Anglos around?" We all laughed.

Jacob was a responsible commissioner during his
brief youthful tenure and now seems to be doing well
in Albuquerque, where he works as a draftsman for
an engineering firm, village kid making good in the
big outside world despite almost overwhelming odds.
I had a passing acquaintance with his father, Elijah, a
crusty, outspoken schoolteacher who tended to render harsh judgment against the newcomer Anglos,
and who once said to me: "You people can come and
go here as often as you like, but those of us who were
born here don't have that choice, we have to stay." A
disappointed lawyer, he had entered the only profes-
sion relatively open to Hispanics at the time—teach-
ing—while running a small practice as a notary out of
his house. Ditch commissioners are supposed to post
a bond, and in my early years as commissioner we
often had Elijah draw up the papers. Ten years ago he
was driving home late one night through the Rio
Grande canyon when he fell asleep or lost control of
his car and went over the edge—though he managed
to climb out of the wreckage before he died. A day
or two after a friend of mine out fishing came across
the body lying on a boulder. His widow, a reclusive
woman, was burdened with the task of raising four
boys by herself. Jacob, the eldest, was fortunately
guided into the hands of a local architect by a neighbor and became an apprentice draftsman as long as
the work lasted, a year of two, and after that he
moved on to the job in Albuquerque. One of the Acequia de la Jara's properties continues to be listed in

Elijah's name at the insistence of his widow, who is now and then given to calling up the ditch treasurer and haranguing whoever it happens to be on such details. Like so many kids in the valley, the three young men in their twenties I am now talking with have had to enter adulthood without a father in the household.

Turning to Mateo and Irwin Serna, I ask them whether either of them might be interested in serving on the commission at the annual meeting to be held about two weeks from now, the first Sunday in March. Irwin, always a bit righteous, voice strained in some undefinable emotion, replies: "I think that's up to the people." "No," I counter, "what I mean is shall I nominate either of you for a position?" Silence. Then Irwin says: "I would be interested." I add that I am willing to be *mayordomo* again. Mateo offers a little humor here: "Like Ferdinand Marcos." We all laugh.

We then launch into a long discussion of the *desagüe* project. I explain to them what I understand of it, that state and federal agencies will pick up 80 percent of the cost and that we can borrow the balance from the Interstate Stream Commission for ten years at 3 percent interest. The money will buy us an upper *desagüe* of steel and concrete, with a head gate we can actually shut off, and constructed strongly enough to survive most floods, plus some kind of lower *desagüe* next to the highway, of a design not yet decided on.

Mateo is skeptical. "Seems like a lot of money to put out for something like that. We could build it our-

selves." We could, yes, I reply, but we wouldn't because we'd never get around to it and wouldn't take
the time or trouble or spend the money to build a
structure that could survive a major flood. I could see
replacing the lower *desagüe* ourselves, but that is a
small job some distance from the river course. I am
somewhat surprised at Mateo's hostility to the project,
but he relents after awhile, perhaps after realizing that
his family's share of the cost will amount to some
$25.00 total, or about $2.50 a year for ten years, as
their place is only one-half *pión.* I have heard that our
ditch is among the last expected to receive funding in
the foreseeable future. There is always a strong pork-
barrel element at the congressional level in this kind of
money, though I see such uses as far more benign and
socially valuable than much of what the military establishment drains from the public purse: we are asking for the cost of a few spare parts on those fighter-
bombers that zoom over our valley on low-altitude
practice runs every two weeks.

With that more or less settled, I urge them to come
to the annual meeting with their questions and doubts,
and then take my leave.

For our county, New Mexico state law specifies
that an *acequia*'s annual meeting is to be held on the
first Monday of December, but we have found March
to be a better time to entice *parciantes* out of their
houses, as by then most people will have begun to

think of plowing their fields and planting their gardens and will be wondering when there will be water in the ditch again. This year Sandra Jackson has reserved the school for two in the afternoon, Sunday, the ninth of March, for our meeting, or rather meetings, since a number of the other ditches will be gathering at the same time. Afterward, the commissions of the various ditches are to set up a schedule of cleaning dates and discuss any other matters they may have in common.

We are all to meet in separate corners of the enormous new gym, on what turns out to be a grey and windy day of wintry cold. An impressively massive structure for a village, the gym was built several years ago at a cost of over a million dollars, but its huge space tends to swallow up individuals in meetings unless everyone is stand–up–and–shouting angry, as was the case during a recent U.S. Forest Service hearing on their long-range forestry plan. Fold-up wooden bleachers along the east wall, electronic scoreboard high up on the west wall, basketball backboards to north and south, bright ceiling floodlights with a color-flattening effect that washes the life out of faces, the space is inhospitable to anything but loud and active sporting events for which it was primarily designed. It was also apparently designed to resemble every other high school gym in America and is perhaps the only place in the village that is identical, like a franchise outlet, to something probably everywhere else in the country and clearly American in a generic sort of way. The only mark of the place, the village, the region, consists of a coiled rattlesnake, the home-team logo, painted in blue and yellow high up in the northwest corner by a local artist.

The half-dozen of us from the Acequia de la Jara gather in the southwest corner and pull up tiny plastic chairs and sit down with knees thrust high and stare up at the frieze of sentimental photo posters in color that runs around the full length of the gym six feet above the floor, posters apparently celebrating and promoting stereotypes of youth, health, agility, "fun," "freedom," "individuality," and so on: young joggers pumping their way through rural midwestern or East Coast or mountain landscapes, photo enlargements of furry animals thought to be cute (rabbits, squirrels, koala bears) or soaring birds seen to embody free-dom, daring, independence—seagulls, hawks, eagles. Perhaps an American Commercial Realism equiva-lent of Russian Social Realism, the posters are num-bered and can be bought by the students—a socially useful introduction to American consumerism—and taken home to display to their culturally regressive Hispanic and dropout Anglo parents. There must be hundreds of different images in the series, which reads like possible scenic backdrops to tobacco or food or automobile commercials shot in some na-tional park of the mind where the air is always clear, the water is clean, and where overeating alternating with exercise has become the great labor of the nation. Knees high, sitting in chairs made for six-year-olds, we scan these icons of middle-class American life, which are about to witness the peculiar proceedings of some of the smallest civic institutions that have ever existed.

There are ten of us here today from the Acequia de la Jara. As usual the Serrano clan is well represented: Ewaldo, ageless, in his seventies, who will receive a murmured translation at critical junctures of the proceedings mostly in English from either his sixty-year-old brother Perfecto, retired miner of studious appearance, or from his brother-in-law Ricardo Serrano, a pleasant fellow in his fifties who rarely misses an annual meeting and always calls for the commission to make delinquent *parciantes* pay or have their water shut off. The brothers Mateo and Irwin Serna have also come, in addition to their neighbor and former commissioner and *mayordomo,* Larry Bustos, who is here today, I imagine, because he's bored this cold and windy March afternoon and is looking for something to do, having happened by the school yard filled with parked cars. In addition to Sandra Jackson, her ex-husband is here, Martin Jackson, and the other commissioner, Arthur Litton. This is the first year I can remember holding a meeting without Ignacio Serna and his hesitantly blurted-out jokes and his clownish laughter now and then running the ritual agenda off on some strange tangent. But in all, this is a good turnout. Perhaps a fourth of our *parciantes* have never come to an annual meeting in my fifteen years here, and roughly another quarter have come only once or twice. Across the echoing expanse of the gym, the second largest ditch in town has only five or so members out of fifty present. In the northwest corner, the Acequia de los Cerritos has attracted a good crowd of around fifteen, or perhaps a third of its membership. Several ditches have still been unable to organize themselves for a meeting even though the space has been provided for that purpose today. The Acequia de las Juntas, largest ditch in town, met at the statutorily correct date last December.

An *acequia* can become an obsession with its *parciantes,* and it is this power of concentration carried to the annual meetings that makes them often unbearably tense. The newcomer can find a first ditch meeting a rude shock, with public displays of personal animosity and heavy-handed manipulation or disregard for procedural niceties that can end up in parking lot scuffles afterward. Such emotional intensity may be tied less to the actual importance of water in people's lives today than the memory of times when it could be a matter of life or death and for which one was beholden via an *acequia* to one's neighbors. Those times have passed, and no one will starve if the river dries up tomorrow, yet the memory of hard times still reaches out of the past. But given the nature of *acequias,* small associations of neighbors and therefore

often of relatives offering at best the slimmest re-
wards, if any, to the politically ambitious, it is rare to
find any one *acequia* tied down by any one individual
or family or faction for more than a few years. *Parciantes* will become heated up for a season or two but
after a time they will lose interest and drift on to something more prestigious or lucrative, or to a group that
involves dealing with people other than neighbors
and relations, and leave the ditch to be run by those
who actually use the water. Years ago, once I had
served as a commissioner for a year or two, my annual reelection came to assume importance in my
mind as a sign of approval by my neighbors, and then
I passed through a phase of believing my position as
commissioner to be essential to my livelihood as a
farmer, and now these past several years I have come
to see that the ditch would probably run quite well
enough in my absence—most years there will be
three or four *parciantes* willing to serve as commissioners and *mayordomo,* and at least one and often two
of them are likely to be halfway responsible. I would
mainly miss the companionship of that long narrow
body of water which my position as *mayordomo* be-
stows on me the right to visit anywhere along its
three-mile length at any time or season.

In her high, melodious voice, Sandra Jackson opens
the meeting with the treasurer's report—we have $250
in the bank, a good sum to begin the season with—
and then brings us up to date on the Soil Conserva-

tion Service *desagüe* projects. Only four *parciantes* not present today have so far failed to return their pooling agreements, and she expects most of them will do so before the deadline. She explains that those who don't sign will have to pay 100 percent of their share of the project, or about $250 per *pión,* as against only about $50 for those who have signed, over the ten-year financing period. After a brief discussion in which everyone seems to be satisfied with the way the paperwork is moving along, Sandra turns to the matter of revising our by-laws to conform to the specifications of the Office of the State Engineer, whose approval is necessary for us to receive the combined state and federal grant in aid that will cover 80 percent or the $10,000 cost. She and Arthur Litton, the other commissioner, have already revised them accordingly and have resubmitted them to the State Engineer. Approval is expected shortly. The ditch probably operated without written by-laws for generations, if not hundreds of years, until about 1974 when Jerry Munster and I, then commissioners, cooked up a set to qualify for emergency aid from the federal government in order to relocate the dam a tenth of a mile downstream to its current and less satisfactory location, following a spring flood that swept away one hundred yards of the channel at the corner of Harold Castillo's orchard. Based in part on sample by-laws in the late Phil Lovato's book, *Las Acequias del Norte,* the by-laws have never been read through by anyone other than lawyers in the State Engineer Office, whose files may well be filled with a thousand other such documents, all perhaps carefully inspected by the state, all perhaps as equally ignored in practice as ours.

Sandra reports that the State Engineer lawyer objected to the date of our annual meeting and stipulated that we are to meet in December, not March, and to our voting by membership, that is, one *parciante,* one vote, instead of by shares, or one *pión,* one vote, as called for by state law. But it is immediately apparent from a flurry of muttered remarks that no one here this afternoon approves of the state-imposed changes. I suggest that we officially accept them while, in fact, continuing to do things the way we always have, particularly to vote by membership. Voting by shares as in a corporation would give the larger landowners more votes, an idea that appears to be offensive to all present—but of course none of our two-*pión parciantes,* Wilfred Ortiz or Paco Ortiz or Gregory Serna, are here today. Someone points out that once we get the *desagües* built and paid for, then we can change the by-laws back the way they were before, an admirable solution.

The meeting is going well. Though minor, matters such as these can often bog down in acrimonious quibbling, with a possibility of consensus becoming increasingly remote. For the cleaning dates, next item on the informal agenda, I propose Tuesday, the eighteenth of March, for cutting the willows, then Thursday and Friday, the twentieth and twenty-first of March, for digging, dates which seem acceptable to everyone. With one or two exceptions when we were snowed out, we have cleaned the ditch the weekend of the vernal equinox. I also urge that we raise the hourly wage to $3.50 for the March cleaning, though not change the rate for summer work crews (who are paid the higher rate of $4.00 an hour). I strongly believe that the raise is essential to hold interest in the ditch by the kids, the teen-agers, who now do most of the actual digging. Better pay also makes it easier for the *mayordomo* to get good work out of the workers, while also depriving them of an excuse to loaf or to be sloppy, which our current $2.50 encourages. I have heard there are ditches in Taos still trying to pay $1.25 an hour and wondering why they fail to attract a good turnout, and if we persist with low wages we will soon find ourselves in the same position. A poor turnout means either that the ditch will be badly cleaned or else that it will take much longer to dig out and thus cost more in both time and money, in the long run. No one objects to the raise.

A special anxiety hovers over small elections among friends and neighbors and relatives, bound together in this case by a narrow channel of water that flows through everyone's backyard, while yet divided by linguistic and cultural differences, plus those of religion, educational background, and so on. And our differences are startling: two of the Anglos here hold

Ph.D.'s and two M.A.'s, while none of the Hispanics have gone beyond high school, and a couple of them may be no more than marginally literate in either Spanish or English. However, what is remarkable about this gathering may be less a matter of such differences than the fact that we are able to sit down together in a roughly oval formation, in tiny plastic chairs, and manage to conduct business together without our differences overcoming that one small thing we have in common, the *acequia*. And the election is a test of the whole delicate arrangement. We all know at some level that we must elect a commission which is not all Anglo or all Hispanic, or all Catholic or Presbyterian, or all from the top of the ditch or the bottom of the ditch, or all Serrano or all Serna. And the meeting does not appear to be stacked in any way—the usual *parciantes* are here, and the ones who usually don't come haven't showed up—and clearly no one has gone around and gathered up *parciantes* in order to put in a new commission; and my own lobbying has consisted of no more than urging Sandra to stay on because she's fiscal agent for the *desagüe* project and Arthur because I regard him as fair and level-headed and aware of the importance of keeping good account records, and of course I have made it known to Irwin Serna that I would like to see him replace his father.

Sandra calls for nominations. Rather than elect each commissioner individually, we will vote on all three together, given the smallness of the group. Irwin turns around and nominates Larry Bustos, and then in quick succession Arthur nominates Sandra, I nominate Irwin, Sandra nominates Arthur, and Larry Bustos nominates Mateo Serna, who declines on the grounds that he is from the same household as his brother Irwin. The Serranos remain aloof from this flurry of politicking. Since my time here they have steadfastly declined to serve on the commission or as *mayordomo*, though Orlando Serrano, not here today, once expressed interest in being *mayordomo* and would probably do well in the position.

In the moment of silence following the nominations, it becomes clear that we have one too many nominees to allow an election by acclamation. Were Robert's Rules of Order or even our own by-laws in effect, half the nominations might be challenged on various grounds, including that two of the nominees are not *parciantes* but sons of *parciantes,* a point that the Acequia de las Juntas, for one, is very picky about. Yet as far as I know, no ditch in the valley has a system of registration whereby a *parciante* must supply proof of the fact through property deeds, for example—an interesting lacuna. A *parciante* is somebody everybody knows is a *parciante* or even finds acceptable as a *parciante*. All our nominees pass the test. The Serrano clan, an inscrutable voting block, will decide the outcome. Arthur Litton begins tearing up sheets of paper into small squares for ballots and then passes them around with an assortment of pencil stubs. At this point Sandra breaks the silence. "If I may say so," she observes thoughtfully, "it might be wise to reelect me since I am the fiscal agent for the *desagüe* project." Arthur turns to her and asks with a laugh: "Is that your campaign speech?" I then interject the comment that, in fact, she can remain as fiscal agent whether or not she is a commissioner, as Jerry Munster did many years ago after failing to be reelected. Since my intention was not at all to cause her to lose, hindsight later informs me that it would have been more politic to have said something after the voting.

So like schoolchildren trying to keep our neighbors from copying, we now furtively scribble out the names on our tiny squares of roughly torn paper. Two of the Serranos, our voting block, step over to the bulletin board where Arthur has posted the four names and study them carefully. In an election where an old-name Hispanic is running against a new-name Anglo, posting the names can make a difference in the outcome, even in a small group of voters who have lived next door to each other for years. Chairs scrape, throats are cleared, words are murmured back and forth between those sitting next to each other, glances are exchanged as the tiny folded ballots are dropped into a cap carried around by Perfecto Serrano, who then takes them over to the bulletin board and unfolds them one by one and reads them out while Arthur tallies the votes next to the four names. In short order, we discover that our new commissioners are Larry Bustos, Irwin Serna, and Arthur again, all winning over Sandra by a couple of votes. Sandra appears bemused by the outcome, not disturbed, and accepts the defeat gracefully.

Next it is my turn to place myself at the mercy of my neighbors in this yearly ritual of judgment, to learn whether I am considered worthy to continue as *mayordomo,* as the one in charge of the water. The fact I have turned up for the meeting declares in part my interest, and there appear to be no other pretenders. Two former *mayordomos* have not turned up, and Irwin and Larry seem content to remain as commissioners. After some generalized bantering at my expense, Arthur declares, "By acclamation, then." Though "by default" might be the better phrase—for this job is not much sought after or envied these days.

We adjourn. The commissioners and I wander over to a group of commissioners from the other ditches huddled over a piece of paper on the bleachers at the far corner, to whom we submit our cleaning date, which is early enough not to conflict with the others. Then we walk out of the gym and the bright stifling light of its echoing cave, its poster photo album of oppressive stereotypes, for the grey outdoors of a real New Mexico—wind, dust, and all.

The occasional snowflake drifts down from a leaden sky as we gather at the upper *desagüe* for what the Soil Conservation Service agent, Jimmy Hollander, calls the "setting of the stakes," the morning of Tuesday, the eighteenth of March. Eight of us in four cars have driven over from Sandra Jackson's house, where we met briefly to discuss funding and contractual matters among the three entities now involved: the federal government, the contractor, and the Acequia de la Jara. Jimmy Hollander is a tall, heavyset man in his late forties, given to wearing plaid shirts, Levis, and cowboy boots. He sports long sideburns down his massive jowls, and his most distinctive feature is the Cheshire Cat smile he flashes on and off as he speaks in a gravelly voice, lightly drawling but also cadenced with touches of Hispanic English. I have had a passing acquaintaince with him for years through various SCS-sponsored meetings and have been into his office a half-dozen times over water- and land-use questions. With him is the SCS engineer, a tall skinny man in his fifties with reddish thinning hair, and scratches on his forehead which suggest he has recently taken a nasty fall in some bushes. At a meeting at Sandra's house a week before, the commission awarded the construction contract to Eric Mondragón, whose bid of $8,000 for the upper *desagüe* was the most professionally presented of the three submitted (which ranged from $7,000 to a strange shot in the dark of $33,000) and included cost breakdowns for concrete, steel gates, and gabions—the large wire baskets to be filled with stones and which will serve as anchoring structures for the concrete work. Mondragón is the builder of the Acequia del Pueblo's monstrous construction near the highway, a bizarre SCS design which he completed with good marks. He has brought his younger brother, assistant in the business, along with him in a bright new Chevy four-wheel-drive pickup, perhaps bought against the anticipated profits of the job. Our two commissioners, Arthur Litton and Irwin Serna, and our fiscal agent, Sandra Jackson, and I rode in the back down through Harold Castillo's orchard, and the six of us now stand around the two government officials squatting down with blueprints spread out on the ditch bank before them, figuring out where the first stake is to be driven.

The engineer picks up a sharpened two-by-four stake and writes "Start Here" in black marker on it, and then he and Hollander place it at the southeast corner of the future structure, next to the trunk of the beaver-felled cottonwood that straddles the ditch, and drive it into the soft sand. That, apparently, is it. As we all stand around in the cold wondering what next, Hollander climbs over the fence and pulls a camera from his car and shoots a couple of pictures of the wintry scene, snowflakes beginning to thicken. For the second shot I place a foot on top of the stake so it will show more clearly in the photo. I call out, "Is this for the government or for history?" "For both," he says with a smile, turning the film. Hollander smiles whenever he speaks, a warm smile or a cold one, a broad and open teeth-baring grin. This is a warm one, and his eyes are alight.

Eleven

Cutting willows and brush satisfies: the feel of the twigs and branches giving between the sharp curved blades of long-handled pruning shears, the low chopping sound as the cut completes, handles squeaking, handles clacking as banged against a fence post or log in this primordial act of culture, clearing land of vegetation, snipping suckers and runners and canes from the banks of an irrigation ditch. One studies the ditch as a form to be restored by trimming, to be reclaimed from the reaching grey tentacles of squawberry bushes whose branches insinuate themselves into neighboring growths of willows, New Mexico olive, juniper, native plum, as they seek to colonize a favored spot along a ditch bank or a roadway, with good southern exposure, to watch (one may imagine) the various traffics of water, of beings, pass by. Related to poison ivy, squawberry's pungent orange berries the size of peppercorns may be used, it is said, for tea; and they, and the whole plant, exude a sharp, dusty sumac-like smell that seems to expand in the nostrils. Tenacious plant, its branches snake along the ground to surface some distance from the tangled central crown, and when you cut them, they cling and snag as you try to pull them free. Squawberry loves barbed-wire fences and must know, if plants know such things, how easy it is to dull one's shears on a strand of wire lying just back of one of the low horizontal branches in the shadows of its dusty, pungent habitation.

During the cutting of the brush, the *acequia* is a pathway not for water but for the dozen of us who file loosely down its meandering course. This morning, Wednesday, the nineteenth of March, last day of winter, crisp and clear and bright with an inch or so of snow which has fallen during the night, we march east to west, downstream, rising sun to our backs. We cut only woody growth, leaving dried clovers, *oshá*, alfalfa, milkweed in their brittle stalks for the crew to hack down tomorrow with shovels, slash down the yellow and brown fringe that lines the ditch banks almost end to end, standing in places three feet high, except where it has been burned off. From the dam down through the open ground of lower pastures of Los Cerritos there is little to cut; cattle and horses and beavers have done this work over the years, and the banks are covered with a lush growth of well-established grasses, offering formidable competition for woodier vegetation. Here and there, every ten or twenty yards, a clump of willows has attempted to establish a toehold low down in the channel, or a cottonwood has sent an exploratory sucker over to our easy source of water, and we shear them back; and junipers line the ditch here on the river side, but they are well-mannered neighbors and do not crowd in, preferring to keep their distance, and we cut them back only where an overhanging branch here and there droops so low it will interfere with tomorrow's digging; nor do I imagine they take much water from us, and indeed, with their shade they may save us more than they tap.

But when the going gets thick one cannot clip without respite, and so after awhile a kind of leap-frogging rhythm evolves as we advance down the ditch in no set formation: the first men of the crew, pressed by those behind, leave most of the brush un-clipped, advancing on ahead to gain some distance, then slowing to clip until once again pressed from behind or stepping aside to let others pass and take the lead for awhile. The taller workers will tend to cut growth along the top of the bank, while the shorter will work on the inside of the channel, low down where the willow and wild rose canes emerge, with everyone off and on browsing in a generalized way the slopes of the middle banks, sometimes cutting thoroughly, sometimes no more than just walking along and looking from side to side and now and then swiping with shears at a tangle of rose canes to make certain they have already been cut. The two or three men bringing up the rear of the crew will cut what the rest have missed, sometimes much, sometimes little, and at a thick concentration of willows or squawberry growth the whole crew will bunch up, the stragglers will catch up, push on ahead, becoming the leaders, leaving the former leaders now to bring up the rear.

Willows encase their dead standing in place, the new canes, sometimes yellow, sometimes a coppery or rusty orange that shows brightly in the snow and whose color ripens with the coming of spring, growing up around to hold and enclose a stand of dead and dying elders, whose grey eight-foot canes curve like bows and can be used as beanpoles, go rotten at the bottom, and sometimes can be pulled up by hand. Tough, sinuous, hard to break, sometimes impossible to cut with pruning shears, the clumps of the standing dead can form a leaning canopy over the ditch, difficult and dusty to work under, as weighed down by a scrambling growth of vines. Willows, somewhat like cottonwoods, live brief, heady existences and will rapidly conquer a strip of wet land and just as rapidly exhaust it of nutrients and die back, leaving a tangled grey ruin that will eventually collapse under the force of wind or snow; but even then, lying old and split on the ground, they will prove too tough to break easily into kindling. Yet a stand of young canes, five and six feet high, late winter or early spring, in a landscape still in the hold of absolutes of snow and ice, can glow with a scarlet warmth and the certain promise of sun returning soon to the earth, and this glow, their knowledge, can ease the human doubt.

Such are the invasive plants, the species that take the most interest in our ditch—plus cottonwoods, of course, with their occasional light grey-green suckers which can spread into a willowlike clump in response to our prunings; but cottonwoods, unless allowed to grow too large to cut back, as has happened a few places along our ditch, are more restrained than willows, having other ways to feed from our labors, in the form of long, tough roots that will grow alongside the channel so thickly on both sides and even the bottom that the ditch cannot be dug out in any direction. Wild roses, intrigued by water but not actually much interested in it, will send up the occasional plum-colored cane whose thorn-spotted variegations make it easy to miss on the bank, and their thorns are long and sharp enough to inspire caution when moving in to nip them at the base; and wild plum and New Mexico olive, both slower growing, will keep a similar distance from the water, preferring to reach over it from above and beneath, as will the odd choke-cherry, apple, or apricot gone to the wild.

We are twelve today, enough in number to clip the banks of the two-mile ditch in the course of this last morning of winter, and the formationless nature of our movement down the channel makes possible long and varied conversations. Aside from now and then urging the crew to clip a little further back on the bank, there is little else I need do except work my clippers along with everybody else. The two Serna brothers are working, in addition to their uncle Ricardo Serna, plus a half-dozen high school kids from across the river who have worked on the ditch before and whose names I have to learn anew each year; and Jake Ortiz, back home from Oregon on his annual vacation and who suggests that we spray a herbicide on the banks of the ditch through the Thompson place where two-foot-high stands of crooked grey fingers, poison oak, reach up out of the humus. Logger that he is, he takes an adversary relation to that alien reality, the natural world: whatever stands must be cut. No, no herbicides, I object, as we cut away: there are too many children and pets and vegetable gardens along here. Poison ivy prefers a rich clay soil, and a degree of shade, and there are stands of it here and there along the ditch, grey stalks with a few pale greenish berries at the top. Most people hereabouts don't seem allergic to it but a few are extremely so, and though my immunity holds I am never comfortable in its presence. Still, the plant is easy to recognize and its effects are known and treatable, which is more than can be said of most herbicides.

Jake Ortiz is Paco Ortiz's younger brother. In his early fifties, a short, dark, muscular man with a nose markedly pushed to one side of a flat round face, and coal black eyes that will settle on you with what can readily be imagined as a murderous stare, and the low growling and rasping voice of the heavy drinker and smoker, he has come back to the valley almost every year in the spring since I have been here for a week or two of heavy drinking, usually around Easter. Between benders fifteen years or so ago, one Saturday morning he walked over from Paco's to our newly built three-room adobe and made the first of a number of memorable appearances in our living room. With little preface, he proceeded to rant and rave at how the ditch had no right to charge him for this or that and how as treasurer I was cheating him, how all of us on the commission plus the *mayordomo* were a bunch of crooks and deserving of some terrible fate. Throughout the spectacular tirade my wife worked quietly away in the kitchen, and in the back room the kids were probably cowering in their bunk beds. I argued, attempting to remain reasonable and calm and not become too angry in the face of the provocations of—it seemed—a dangerous madman, and after a quarter of a hour of this, quite as suddenly as he had begun, he calmed down and decided that everything was all right, and by the time he was ready to leave in another half hour, he was heartily anxious to prove that he thought me a fine fellow, that we were to be best friends, that he was going to pay his *delincuencias* just as soon as he could. The change of heart had less to do with what I said or did (or refrained from) than from the fact of his being able so wonderfully to vent his spleen without apparently damaging effects and no grudge held against him. A year or so later he gave a repeat performance in our living room, though we got to the best-friends stage much more rapidly—and yes, of course he would pay his *delincuencias,* every penny, because he was fair and wanted to do his part and be a good neighbor, even though he never used the water and had a low opinion of almost everybody on the ditch. Several years later when Sandra Jackson became treasurer she called me one morning late in the spring and asked in a breathless, panicked voice: "Who is this Jake Ortiz?" I explained that, in fact, he was quite all right but that you had to endure a half hour of verbal abuse to reach the point where you could see what a fine fellow he was; sorry I had failed to warn her. "Oh my god," she said, "I have never been through anything like it."

By midmorning the sun is trying to come out and the snow has mostly melted. We have worked rapidly through the jungly growth of the Serna place, going back and cutting it twice in places, and the rest of the morning, cool enough to work pleasantly in, passes quickly. Irwin thinks we ought to dig this afternoon, after lunch, and the others seem willing, but I decide it would mess up the roll call and bookkeeping and that I would rather start tomorrow according to our original plan.

We finish the lower half of the ditch some time after twelve noon, and I write out *papelitos* for five hours. Most of us have to walk most of the way back up the ditch to our houses or cars, and by the time we have eaten lunch it will be almost two. My suggestion to call it a day is assented to by Irwin without objection now. Everyone is a little tired. The day is trying to clear, and by tomorrow perhaps the weather will be at last dry and sunny.

I walk back up the road with Jake Ortiz, who is staying with his brother again two doors down from us. In his gravelly voice he rattles on about his divorce—last time he was back here he came with his new wife—and the automated tree-harvesting equipment that has cost him his job in Oregon, though he is still able to find enough part-time work to keep him busy, and about the hybrid super-trees that are supposed to change everything but about which he is skeptical. "Hell," he says. "I've been there as long as those things, twenty-five years, and they're not doing so hot."

The collective power of a ditch crew of twenty or thirty men can often be felt as threatening or dangerous, but what holds it in restraint are the conventions and traditions that have evolved out of hundreds of years of maintaining *acequias*—a complex social fabric binds a ditch crew together far more than the character of a *mayordomo* or the commissioners, recalling it

to a sense of common purpose and preventing the in-
evitable disputes from flaring into political divisive-
ness or even physical violence. And there is also something almost comical in the often ragged band of a
ditch-cleaning crew—many of us wear old clothes,
knowing that the thirty barbed-wire fences we climb
over and under and through each day will take their
toll on jackets and shirts and jeans, boots will become
caked with mud, clothes can be blackened by charred
branches and limbs, and on dry and windy days we
can find ourselves repeatedly bathed by blowing dust
and silt. And often the crew will become a little wild-
eyed and haggard with fatigue, and as they dig, bent
over nearly double, the younger boys will be dwarfed
by the long shovel handles sticking out of their backs
between elbows and ribs, nearly vertical, taller than
their bent heads. Ditch-cleanings are all very much
the same, and in this they often feel more like ritual
than work. The crew varies from year to year: a couple
of old men don't turn up each year, a couple of boys
barely able to handle a shovel, fifteen- and sixteen-
year-olds, take their places; the weather is better or
worse than some vague notion of what is usual, *mayordomos* come and go and some are responsible and
fair, others vindictive, punitive, almost military, others are lazy and heedless of the needs of the ditch; and
the crew can be a good-natured, hard-working creature, or sullen and complaining and evasive, qualities

perhaps dictated by the amount of pride or fear circulating through the hearts of both those in charge and those doing the actual digging. And a ditch crew always looks much the same when it is at work, with thirty or so men spread out along some two hundred feet of a knee-deep ditch channel, with half the men and boys bent over double and then every few seconds standing up straight to fling a shovelful of dirt or sand or gravel up onto a bank to either side, then looking briefly up or down the line, smoothing back hair, readjusting a cap, jackets and sweatshirts tied around their waists, with the workers at the head of the line, their *tareas* done, stnding with hands folded over the tops of their shovel handles as they chat and joke or smoke or kick at the sand in the bottom of the ditch or scrape the mud from their shovel blades with a stick, while waiting for the rest of the crew to finish.

The digging that begins at the top of the ditch at eight A.M., Thursday, the twentieth of March, 1986, the first day of spring, following one of the last nights Halley's Comet can be seen, and that ends a day and a half later is little different from the digging of the year before or any of the other fifteen years I have been involved in the task: a good crew of thirty men both days, most of whom I have worked with as *mayordomo* now for three years, which means that we both know what to expect from each other, and consequently the work seems to progress faster and more easily than usual. The days are beautiful: clear, windless, yet not warm enough to inspire springtime lethargies except in the odd protected spot where the sun focuses its heat and where the earth and the leafless bushes send out the fragrances that herald a renewal of growth. Irwin Serna and Larry Bustos have suggested that as commissioners they take turns pacing off the *tareas* with the *vara,* which is actually less an innovation than a return to a more traditional practice, so that I can keep track of the names and more easily inspect the line. The first day Irwin does the pacing off, though somewhat erratically and without rhythm and too much looking back and forth, frowning under the weight of his new responsibility, yet still managing to dole out more or less equal *tareas;* and the second morning Larry confidently takes over and strides rapidly and evenly down the line, shouting out the numbers, and then takes a position up on the bank with the *vara* planted upright in place and where he smokes a cigar and amuses the workers with a patter of jokes and puns in Spanish, which too is part of the tradition, the ritual.

Two of our elders do not show up this year: Reynaldo Vasques, one-time *mayordomo,* next to the last *parciante* on the ditch, and who had heart surgery early in the year; and Ewaldo Serrano, down with the flu; and after Orlando Serrano, who looks older and tired this year and works in uncharacteristic silence, I find myself now the oldest, nearing fifty, suddenly an elder or almost so. But there are new faces, younger brothers to kids probably working their last season on the ditch before going off to college or a job in Los Alamos or Santa Fe or Albuquerque, plus this year, for the first time, speakers of other kinds of Spanish: Marcos Quintana, a Puerto Rican friend of mine, down from Taos where he has recently settled, a radical actor-activist curious about this pocket of Third World activity; and Manuel of Chihuahua, a shy young man in his twenties who, bewildered and excited by the unfamiliar labor, forgets his number most of the first morning and repeatedly leaves his lunch sack behind, until he finally settles into the rhythm of the work and feels at ease among us. And then there are the usual characters who always show up, as if they are handed down from generation to generation along with the traditions of the ditch itself: Tito Pacheco, a portly forty-five-year-old with jutting teeth who survives on odd jobs in the valley and who complains each year that his *tareas* are always longer than anyone else's, as indeed they may well be: there is something in his perennial complaints that seems to bring on the affliction then complained of; and first he complains to his neighbors, then he complains to me that Irwin is giving him *tareas* longer than anyone else's, and then I see him standing on the bank pleading with Irwin no doubt to reduce the length of his *tareas,* and through all this he doubtless fails to see that if he were not so obsessed with the size of his *tareas* and were more concerned with the task, in which sometimes you help your two neighbors finish their sometimes more difficult *tareas,* and sometimes your neighbors help you finish yours when it proves difficult, he would understand that as always the length of one's *tarea* is to an extent always in the mind.

Or that this small thing, this two-pace-long-by-four-feet-wide area, the size of a large bathtub, a grave, can be a source of great pride, as it is for Buddy Manzanares who, on one of my last perfunctory inspection tours half an hour from the end of the spring digging, calls on me to admire a meticulously dug out and cleaned up *tarea,* with the banks cleaned of grass and squared neatly where they end in the bottom of the smoothly shoveled-out channel. "Look at that *tarea,*" he stutters out, beaming. Buddy is a handsome forty-five-year-old whose dashing boyish looks and tattooed arms with bulging muscles cohabit the lined face and sagging beer-belly of the aging warrior, and whose hearty "Hello, my friend!" at the post office or store I first found irritating—until I realized how genuinely effusive the man is. "Look at that *tarea.* Isn't that good work?" "Yes," I nod, "*muy suave.*" Larry Bustos, standing above on the bank with his pole and Swisher Sweet, calls down in his deep rumbling voice, loud enough that all can hear: "A masterpiece of a *tarea!*" We all laugh, Buddy too: yes, this man knows how to make this small thing, this chore, into more than we commonly imagine, and what can be more important to know in this life, than just that. And we laugh for once not in mockery but in delight. . . .

For Further Reading

Acequias y Sangrias, Guidebook to Photo Exhibit. Albuquerque: Southwest Hispanic Research Institute of the University of New Mexico, 1986.

Cobos, Ruben. *A Dictionary of New Mexico and Southern Colorado Spanish*. Santa Fe: Museum of New Mexico Press, 1983.

Glick, Thomas F. *Irrigation and Society in Medieval Valencia*. Cambridge, Mass.: The Belknap Press of Harvard University Press, 1970.

Lovato, Phil. *Las Acequias del Norte*. Taos: Four Corners Regional Commission, 1974.

Meyer, Michael C. *Water in the Hispanic Southwest*. Tucson: University of Arizona Press, 1984.

231